CHRIST CENTERED DATING

PURSUING A RELATIONSHIP THAT GLORIFIES GOD

CHRIST CENTERED DATING

MARK BALLENGER

DAVID C COOK
transforming lives together

CHRIST-CENTERED DATING
Published by David C Cook
4050 Lee Vance Drive
Colorado Springs, CO 80918 U.S.A.

Integrity Music Limited, a Division of David C Cook
Brighton, East Sussex BN1 2RE, England

Library of Congress Control Number 2022941705
ISBN 978-0-8307-8450-9
eISBN 978-0-8307-8451-6

The Team: Michael Covington, Kevin Scott,
James Hershberger, Jack Campbell, Susan Murdock
Cover Design: John Lucas

Printed in the United States of America
First Edition 2023

1 2 3 4 5 6 7 8 9 10

102122

To everyone who has interacted with my online content at ApplyGodsWord.com—serving you has been one of the greatest blessings in my life. Thank you for the abundance of encouragement and support you have shown me over the years.

Applying God's word with you,

Mark

CONTENTS

Introduction

UNITING DESIRES

You probably picked up this book because it is about dating. My hope, though, is that it is first about how to glorify God.

In these pages, my goal has been to marry the two topics "how to date" and "how to glorify God." You can think of it as a book about "how to glorify God through your pursuit of marriage."

God's glory must be at the center of all we do, including relationships.

A few years ago, I started sharing online some of my ideas about how to apply the word of God to the pursuit of marriage. I thought my videos might help a few dozen people who happened to stumble upon them. I had no idea this content would resonate with so many people. At the time of my writing this book, the videos I've posted online have received over 80 million views.

It appears some people enjoy my teaching style and how I help them apply the word of God to relationships. But I believe a big part of the reason for my videos' popularity is a deep thirst among Christian singles for a biblical perspective on the pursuit of marriage.

Christian content for singles who desire marriage has too often created a divide between the desire to glorify God and the desire to date. The primary message has been "Just focus on God. Be content. God will give you your spouse when it's time." That may not be bad advice, but it is woefully incomplete. When a single person longs both to please God *and* to be married one day, such guidance can feel like a slap in the face. The unfortunate response is often "Forgive me, God, for not being content. I'm sorry for wanting to be married. I just can't help it."

Many people have told me how grateful they were that I showed them through Scripture that the choice between pursuing God and pursuing marriage is not either-or. You don't need to stuff down your desire for a godly spouse to avoid offending God's sensitivity about your desires for him. God is secure. He knows his place in your life. Remember, God is the one who made marriage (Gen. 2) and gives the desire for marriage (1 Cor. 7:7). Singles don't need to pick God *over* a relationship but put God first *in* a relationship.

One of the key perspectives of this book is that you don't need to make a choice between glorifying God and pursuing a relationship. Putting God before your desire for marriage pits God and marriage against each other, which is not what God wants. It is much better to intentionally marry the two goals together.

Rather than putting God before your desire for a relationship, God wants you to put him first in your desire for a relationship.

Everything we do as Christians must be for the glory of God, and this truth must also be applied to our desire and pursuit of marriage.

If we truly believe what the Bible says about the glory of God—that everything should be done to bring Christ maximum honor (1 Cor. 10:31; Col. 3:17)—then the lack of Christian content on reflecting God's glory in dating is a major oversight.

One objection I often receive is "Why do you talk about relationships so much? You should talk about more important things like the gospel, sin, and how to obey God."

My initial answer to this complaint is that the internet is a big place. I don't feel pressured to talk about every important topic, because God has blessed many other people with the gift of teaching too. If you need help learning about the gospel and other core biblical truths, there are plenty of ministries available to you. There are fewer people, however, talking about the topics I discuss. So consider mine a ministry that comes alongside churches that can't always get into the weeds with Christian singles seeking marriage.

On a deeper level, however, I think this complaint reveals a flaw in thinking that hurts single people in our churches: believing that the topic of Christian dating is trivial. Many pastors don't want to be relegated to the "JV team" and talk about dating when they could be "varsity" and talk about marriage.

Rather than putting God before your desire for a relationship, God wants you to put him first in your desire for a relationship.

Yet many married Christians carry regret for a season of sin in their relationships when they were single. If so much pain can flow from handling these relationships improperly, shouldn't we invest the time and biblical rigor of study to learn how to honor God while we're in them? If marriage is so important, as the Bible makes clear, shouldn't we carefully lay the best possible foundation before marriage?

While the topic of dating is truly not as significant as the gospel, prayer, Bible study, obedience, and so on, dating can be one of the major playing fields where our beliefs influence our actions. For example, who you choose to date reflects your understanding of the gospel. Your ability or inability to resist sin will impact your dating relationship. And if you are going to disobey and turn from God in singleness, the temptations that lead to your backsliding will likely involve your relationship desires.

Most of the time when pastors teach about singleness and relationships, they do so in a lighthearted, shallow way—with lots of jokes, stories, and personal opinions. While I try to sprinkle in humor, share my personal story about dating my wife, Bethany, and give my opinions, I hope this book offers much more—a serious study about God's glory and your pursuit of marriage *from a biblical perspective.*

The question I seek to answer is, What does the Bible say about pursuing marriage? This topic is often ignored because the Bible doesn't speak directly to it at any length. Thus, Christian singles are often left with little more than various opinions within the Christian community. We need to prayerfully and wisely apply relevant scriptural principles that help us pursue marriage in a biblical way.

This book is not for the youth group, but for the Christian adult who silently prays for a spouse. It is for those who want a serious study about Scripture's view on relationships before marriage. It is for those who are single, who desire to honor the Lord, and who want to be married one day.

With that target audience in mind, please note that my emphasis on glorifying God in the pursuit of marriage is not meant to discourage anyone from pursuing a life of singleness, if that is their desire and calling. I'm not suggesting that you can glorify God in marriage more than you can in singleness. As Paul said, "Each has his own gift from God, one of one kind and one of another" (1 Cor. 7:7). I'm simply focusing on those who are intentionally pursuing marriage rather than a life of singleness. My goal is not to convince all Christians they should pursue marriage, but to offer guidance to those who want to be married.

While the steps in this book can be followed in a logical and practical way that will get you results, please understand that I am not offering a "formula to find the one." While, in a sense, I do believe in the idea of "the one" (see chapter 5), I do not believe in a one-size-fits-all approach to meeting, dating, and marrying the one God has for you. If God wanted all Christians to meet and marry their spouse in the exact same way, he would have given us a step-by-step blueprint in the Bible.

Rather than giving us a treasure map leading to marriage, God has provided us with principles to apply in our pursuit of marriage. I've arranged the study of these principles into three main sections. Section 1 focuses on preparing internally (your heart) to glorify God in your pursuit of marriage. Section 2 evaluates the pre-dating steps necessary to enter into a godly relationship. Section 3 looks at dating in a biblical way once you have met someone.

I am truly honored and excited to walk this journey with you. Let's dive into section 1 and start laying a biblical foundation for our goal of glorifying God through your pursuit of marriage.

Section One

How to Prepare Your Heart to Glorify God in Your Pursuit of Marriage

1

CHAOS TO ORDER

"When in Rome," I muttered to myself as I gleefully took another cupcake from the dessert tray.

I heard a little chuckle from behind me. The line was from a comedy that was popular at the time, and I was purposely using it out of context, in a way that didn't really make sense, to amuse myself. So I had to wonder who had felt compelled to laugh at my nonsense.

It turned out to be my future wife, Bethany, and this was the start to our first significant social interaction. We had both been serving on a mission trip in Liberia with the Mercy Ships organization, which uses hospital ships to offer medical assistance to those in need. We had been introduced in passing, but our ship had over four hundred crew members, and we had not yet had a chance to get to know each other.

We were at the birthday party of a mutual friend when I snatched the extra cupcake.

"Oh, sorry," I said as I turned with an embarrassed smile. "I didn't think anyone could hear me. It was a joke from a movie."

"I know," she said, smiling back. "It's just funny that you made a joke out loud to yourself. Who does that?" She started laughing again. I wasn't sure if she was laughing with me or at me. Either way, I didn't care. I was hooked.

As we talked, we discovered we both had the same favorite Christian author and other common interests as well. Before long, the people around us seemed to disappear. All I cared about was knowing everything about Bethany, and for some reason, she felt the same way about me. Then …

She gasped with a slight tinge of disgust. "Oh, you're nineteen!" She quickly regained her composure and said, "That's cool. I'm twenty-four."

Nothing more was said about our age difference, and we both retreated to the relative safety of the "friend zone." We became great friends in the remaining five months of the mission trip, probably because we didn't feel pressure to be anything more. Fresh out of high school and talking to a pretty registered nurse, I considered romance a pipe dream.

After the mission trip was over, we stayed in touch—emailing each other almost daily, talking on the phone every few weeks, and trying to find excuses to see each other while acting like it was "just a friend thing." It was becoming something more, however, and when I turned twenty—and lost that annoying "teen" at the end of my age—I decided to shoot my shot.

"So …," I said over the phone one night. I had rehearsed this moment a lot, but I felt myself freezing up. *Just do it, Mark. Don't be a wimp. It's time.*

"I, uh … well, I think it's pretty obvious you and me have gotten really close lately. I feel like it's time for me to get in or out with you, because I don't want to play games with your heart or our friendship to be too intimate."

Bethany later said she thought I would tell her we should take a step back because I had started college and we were in different seasons of life. That's not where I was going.

"I've been praying a lot about it. I mean, so I want you to have time to think and pray about it too—but I want to know if you would be my girlfriend. I really like you and want to commit more to you than friendship can offer. What do you think?"

"Yes," she said quickly.

"Oh, wow! I mean—don't you want to pray about it first?"

"I already have," she said. "I knew I would date you if you asked me, but I thought you wouldn't because of our age difference."

"Yeah, I wasn't sure how you felt about that. There may be challenges, but now that I'm twenty, I thought maybe I had a small chance with you."

She laughed and agreed that telling her friends she was dating a nine*teen*-year-old was a bit much.

We dated long distance for a year before she moved from North Carolina to Cleveland, Ohio, where I was finishing up college. Four months later, we were engaged, and four months after that, we were married.

The Center of Your Story

That's a quick snapshot of our story. We've been married since 2008 and created countless more memories together. Some are fun to think about; some are painful. There have been lots of failures and wins, arguments and bliss, hurtful words and loving words, forgiveness, maturing, growing intimacy, laughter with our two kids, parental stresses, ministry, and God's amazing grace. And I'm sure many more highs and lows are to come.

Of all the people who have ever lived, no one has a relationship story exactly like mine. Not that mine is special. Quite the opposite! And if you asked everyone who has ever been married to share their story, each story would have unique details that differ from everyone else's. So if God blesses you with a marriage one day, your journey will be beautifully unique as well.

Perhaps that's why the Bible doesn't give a lot of detail about the pre-marriage process. If God wanted us all to have the same experiences in our relationships leading up to marriage, he might have outlined a much more rigid system in the Bible. But he didn't.

So how will we figure out what God wants us to do in our pursuit of marriage, if the Bible has little to say about dating? Don't get me wrong. I like sharing stories from my life, and I will, but our stories are not authoritative truth. If we base principles on personal experiences, we may lead others astray when their personal experiences differ from ours. Even if I could write an enjoyable book based entirely on Bethany's and my experience, it would not be as helpful as one containing eternal truths that are relevant for everyone all the time.

There are countless questions and issues that are not specifically addressed in the Bible. The Bible is not an encyclopedia in which we can look up every random topic—even the important ones—and find the information we're seeking. God has not provided a heavenly search engine that spits back divine answers to every question we ask. However, we can find everything we need to know to accomplish God's will in Scripture.

God did not provide a formula for dating; instead, he gave us eternal truth that can shape every part of our lives—including our pursuit of marriage.

There is one major theme in Scripture that seems to arc over every other theme, unifying everything: the glory of God. Everything, including the seasons you go through in your journey toward marriage, is meant to bring glory to God.

God's glory links your story and mine. Some people are called to a life of singleness and others to a life of marriage. Those called to marriage each meet their spouse in a different way. And each has unique joys and pains throughout their relationship experience. But after studying the Bible, I am absolutely convinced that everything, for all of us, swirls around the glory of God.

God did not provide a formula for dating; instead, he gave us eternal truth that can shape every part of our lives—including our pursuit of marriage.

So, before we can talk about how to glorify God through your pursuit of marriage, we first need to unpack what it means to glorify God.

Glorifying God

Moses stood before the manifest presence of God. He had God's full attention. As he stood on the mountaintop before his Creator, he could have requested anything. What did he ask?

> Moses said, "Please show me your glory." And [God] said, "I will make all my goodness pass before you and will proclaim before you my name 'The LORD.'" (Ex. 33:18–19)

"The glory of God" is such a common phrase in Christian vocabulary that we can miss its significance. We must fight to keep this important phrase from getting sucked into our vocabulary bank of meaningless religious platitudes. If we lose the meaning of "God's glory," meaninglessness will trickle down to every area of our lives.

Removing God's glory from the center of your being is like removing an engine from a car. It's like removing your heart from your chest. It's like removing love from a marriage. You lose the whole point of your Christian faith. As 1 Corinthians 10:31 commands, "So, whether you eat or drink, or whatever you do, do all to the glory of God."

Moses understood this, which is why his request was so pleasing to God. God granted Moses' request to see his glory, saying, "I will make all my goodness pass before you and will proclaim before you my name 'The LORD.'" Therefore, we can conclude:

God's glory is when God's goodness and character are made known to the watching world.

The phrase "made known" means God is revealing himself in a visible or knowable way. Bible names, in the Old Testament especially, are more than identifying labels. They carry information about a person's character and essence. When God said he would proclaim his name before Moses, he meant that he was going to make his character and essence known to him.

By examining a handful of other biblical examples, we can confirm that this is what is most often meant by the phrase "God's glory" in Scripture.

When Isaiah saw the Lord sitting on his throne, he heard the seraphim singing, "Holy, holy, holy is the LORD of hosts; the whole earth is full of his glory!" (Isa. 6:3). We might have expected the second line of this song to say "the whole earth is full of his holiness!" But when the holiness of God fills the earth in a visible or knowable way, it is referred to as "his glory."

When God visibly displayed his power (as in the cloud filling the temple) or performed a miracle (like providing manna from heaven), it was often said that the glory of the Lord appeared (Ex. 40:34; 2 Chron. 5:14; Ex. 16:7–10). The character and power of God were on display.

When God made the earth and everything in it, he did so to display aspects of himself. Everything created by God reflects something about him, as Psalm 19:1–4 states:

> The heavens declare the glory of God,
> and the sky above proclaims his handiwork.
> Day to day pours out speech,
> and night to night reveals knowledge.

> There is no speech, nor are there words,
> whose voice is not heard.
> Their voice goes out through all the earth,
> and their words to the end of the world.

Creation speaks a language every human can understand, regardless of nationality or geographical location. When you see the sky, it "pours out speech" about God. Thus, "the heavens declare the glory of God."

When God is made known through creation, it's called *glory*. For this reason, no one who denies God has an excuse. He made himself known in the world where we live. Romans 1:20–25 explains:

> For his invisible attributes, namely, his eternal power and divine nature, have been clearly perceived, ever since the creation of the world, in the things that have been made. So they are without excuse. For although they knew God, they did not honor him as God or give thanks to him, but they became futile in their thinking, and their foolish hearts were darkened. Claiming to be wise, they became fools, and exchanged the glory of the immortal God for images resembling mortal man and birds and animals and creeping things.
>
> Therefore God gave them up in the lusts of their hearts to impurity, to the dishonoring of their bodies among themselves, because they exchanged

> the truth about God for a lie and worshiped and served the creature rather than the Creator, who is blessed forever! Amen.

God's "invisible attributes" can be "clearly perceived" by observing his creation. When people rejected these truths, they "exchanged the glory of the immortal God" as well as "the truth about God for a lie." The two phrases mean essentially the same thing. When God made his "invisible attributes" visible and the "truth about God" knowable, he revealed his "glory." Thus, when people rejected the visible truth about God in creation, they rejected God's glory.

Theologians refer to nature as God's "general revelation," while they refer to Scripture as God's "special revelation." God reveals himself in a general way to all people through creation, and in a special and specific way through the illumination of Scripture by the Holy Spirit. But when people deny the truths about God in the Bible, like they deny the truths about God in creation, they (again) miss God's glory: "for all have sinned and fall short of the glory of God" (Rom. 3:23).

Sin occurs when we disobey God's commands. But what if God said adultery was good; would adultery be good? If God said murder was fine, would murder be fine? If God said lying was okay, would lying be okay?

When you understand God's laws, questions like these are nonsense. God's laws are not a list of random rules he picked out of thin air. Rather, they reflect his nature. God commanded faithfulness in marriage, because God is faithful. God said murder is a sin, because

God is just. God commands truthfulness, because God is true. The laws of God make known God's invisible nature.

So asking if adultery, murder, or lying would be good if God said so is like asking, "Would God be different if he was different?" God's laws reflect who God is. The only way God could have given different laws would be if God were different than he is. God gave us the laws we have because they reflect his unchanging nature. His word and moral laws will never change, because they reflect him, and he never changes (Ps. 119:89; 1 Pet. 1:25; Heb. 13:8).

This is why, when we look at the law, it is like looking at a mirror that shows us our flaws (James 1:23–24; Rom. 3:20). We were made in God's image (Gen. 1:27), but when we look at the perfect image of God reflected in the law, we see that, because of sin, our reflection of God's image is no longer fully accurate. The law shows us that our image-bearing is flawed, because we no longer match the picture of God's character revealed in his laws. Only Jesus can reflect God's character perfectly, which is why only Jesus could fulfill the law perfectly (Matt. 5:17).

In Romans 3:23, we might expect something like "for all have sinned and fall short of obeying God's commands." But instead, it says sin causes us to "fall short of the glory of God." The word *sin* literally means "to miss the mark." When we sin, we are missing the mark of accurately reflecting his image. When we reveal God accurately, we reflect his glory. When we conceal God, it's called sin (we "fall short of his glory"). When God's truth about himself is made known through his laws, the Bible calls this "the glory of God."

This same truth can be seen in God's creation of humans. Genesis 1:27 says, "So God created man in his own image, in the image of

God he created him; male and female he created them." Similarly, Isaiah 43:6–7 says, "Bring my sons from afar and my daughters from the end of the earth, everyone who is called by my name, whom I created for my glory, whom I formed and made." God created us for his glory, thus God created us in his image. When we reflect his invisible qualities in a visible way, it's called glory. Through the gospel, God is bringing himself glory by restoring his image in us through Christ (Col. 1:27). As 2 Corinthians 3:16–18 says:

> But when one turns to the Lord, the veil is removed. Now the Lord is the Spirit, and where the Spirit of the Lord is, there is freedom. And we all, with unveiled face, beholding the glory of the Lord, are being transformed into the same image from one degree of glory to another. For this comes from the Lord who is the Spirit.

As we are being transformed into God's true image, we reveal his glory by increasing degrees, because God's glory is manifest when his image is revealed.

This truth about God's glory can be seen most clearly in the person and work of Jesus Christ. If I were to ask, "What person has glorified God the most in all of human history?" Certainly, the answer is Jesus Christ. But why?

Jesus glorifies God the most because he reveals God the most. Jesus is the God-Man, which means he is God and thus has given us a perfectly accurate and visible representation of God. As Colossians 1:15 says, "He is the image of the invisible God." John 1:14, 18 says:

> The Word became flesh and made his dwelling among us. We have seen his glory, the glory of the one and only Son, who came from the Father, full of grace and truth....
>
> No one has ever seen God, but the one and only Son, who is himself God and is in closest relationship with the Father, has made him known. (NIV)

John said we have "seen his glory" and that Jesus made the Father known to us. Jesus glorified God perfectly and to the maximum, because he made God visible and knowable to us. Hebrews 1:3 says Jesus "is the radiance of the glory of God and the exact imprint of his nature." Jesus revealed God to us, and this is seen most clearly in the gospel. Notice the powerful connection between God's glory and the gospel of Jesus Christ:

> In their case the god of this world has blinded the minds of the unbelievers, to keep them from seeing the light of the gospel of the glory of Christ, who is the image of God. For what we proclaim is not ourselves, but Jesus Christ as Lord, with ourselves as your servants for Jesus' sake. For God, who said, "Let light shine out of darkness," has shone in our hearts to give the light of the knowledge of the glory of God in the face of Jesus Christ. (2 Cor. 4:4–6)

The phrase "seeing the light of the gospel of the glory of Christ, who is the image of God" can be confusing to follow. I've found it helpful to start backward to understand what this is saying. Beginning with "God," we see that Jesus is the image of God and thus reveals the most about God. Then we learn that the gospel reveals the most about Jesus. The gospel gives us light to see who Jesus is, and Jesus in turn reveals who God is. If God's glory is God revealed, the apex expression of God's glory is the gospel of Jesus Christ.

Jesus Christ and his gospel reveal more about God than anything else ever could. Therefore, when you read 2 Corinthians 4:6, you find the phrase "the light of the knowledge of the glory of God in the face of Jesus Christ." Jesus Christ and his gospel glorify God most because they reveal God the most. Everything you need to know about his glory, everything God wants you to know about his glory, can be seen in Jesus.

We started with the question "What does it mean to glorify God?" If God's glory is God's goodness and character revealed in a visible or knowable way, and if Jesus Christ reveals God's goodness and character the most, the answer to our question is:

To glorify God, you must make Jesus known.

If you want to glorify God in dating, Christ must be at the center of your dating—hence the title of this book, *Christ-Centered Dating: Pursuing a Relationship That Glorifies God.*

Glorifying God in Pursuit of Marriage

Now, applying what we've learned about glorifying God to our questions about the pursuit of marriage, we can say:

If we want to glorify God through our pursuit of marriage, our goal is to reflect Jesus at all times.

Our goal throughout the Christian dating process is the same as our overall goal as Christians—to live like Jesus. Of course, Jesus was a single man who lived in ancient Israel, so your experience will be much different than his. But as Christians, we can invite the Holy Spirit to fill us so that our character, actions, and attitude resemble Jesus' character, actions, and attitude. As Philippians 2:5 commands, "In your relationships with one another, have the same mindset as Christ Jesus" (NIV).

In applying these truths specifically to romantic relationships, we are led to Ephesians 5:21–33, where Paul described the imagery God intended a Christian marriage to express.

A Christian husband and wife are called to reflect Christ and his bride, the church. Ephesians 5:31–32 says, "'Therefore a man shall leave his father and mother and hold fast to his wife, and the two shall become one flesh.' This mystery is profound, and I am saying that it refers to Christ and the church."

That last phrase—"it refers to Christ and the church"—leads us to the heart of what I hope to express in this book.

If you want to glorify God in dating, Christ must be at the center of your dating.

Keep in mind that the verse says marriage refers to Christ and the church, not vice versa. Sometimes Christian singles have fallen victim to a subtle bait and switch, in which they have been led to believe that "glorifying God" is sort of a prerequisite for finding a Christian spouse. "Give God glory, and God will give you a marriage," so the logic has gone.

What I hope to show you is that the opposite is true. If God has called you to pursue marriage, he has done so that you might, in turn, glorify him (i.e., make his goodness known) through your marriage relationship. Glorifying God is not the admission price to a loving marriage; it is the result of loving your spouse well in marriage!

It's essential to get the order right. Christ and the church do not point to marriage; marriage points to Christ and the church (Eph. 5:32). God is not there to serve marriage; marriage is there to serve God. Glorifying God doesn't lead to the goal of marriage; your future marriage helps achieve the goal of glorifying God. When Christian singles are taught the wrong order, as so often happens, chaos ensues.

But when you get the order right—when you stop trying to use your service and love for God as leverage to get a healthy relationship—you unlock the secret to a godly relationship. Healthy relationships are by-products of God-centered lives, not the other way around.

If you worship God rather than your personal happiness, you will accomplish both. If you worship your personal happiness rather than God, you will accomplish neither. The same is true when it comes to relationships. If you seek to glorify God so he will give you a relationship, you will not truly glorify God, and your relationships will not function properly. But if you seek to use your relationships to bring glory to God, he will be glorified, and your relationships will function much better.

When you order God's glory properly in your heart, the rest of your life will come into order as well. Things work best when we use them as they were designed. And if relationships were made to glorify God, that means your relationships will be at their healthiest when they are being used in this way. This same principle applies to your pursuit of marriage as well.

2

YOUR "WHY" CONTROLS YOUR "HOW"

"Do you want to go on a night hike?"

I knew exactly how Bethany would answer. Early on, her dad instilled in her a love for nature by taking their family on various outdoor adventures and camping trips. I too was raised to love the outdoors, so most of our dates consisted of hiking, rock climbing, or creek walking. While a night hike was a little out of the norm for us, I had a surprise planned for this special date.

When we arrived at Tinker's Creek, our favorite hike in northeast Ohio, the parking lot was empty and the moon was bright, with not a cloud in the sky. The air was cool but refreshing. We wore winter hats, long-sleeve shirts, and light jackets. So far, my prayers for the perfect setting were being answered.

The path stretched alongside a softly flowing creek, glistening with moonlight. You could hear water trickling over the small rock falls in the creek bed.

As we talked, my mind was already a mile down the trail at a little waterfall. I kept praying that this time together would be special for us. Suddenly, two great blue herons glided together down the middle of the creek near us, just a few feet above the water's surface.

"Wow!" Bethany exclaimed. "Did you see that? That was so pretty!"

Thank you, Lord, I thought. *That was really kind of you.* Seeing those two majestic birds flying together felt like a small blessing from the Lord—something I couldn't have planned. It made the hike feel special, even though the most important thing hadn't happened yet.

The moonlight enhanced the little waterfall's beauty. When we arrived, we found a nice sitting rock near the water's edge to take in the scene around us. Now was the perfect time.

"Well, I have to confess, I brought you here to talk about something. Like I said when we started dating, I don't want to waste time playing games. My goal was never to just date you. I wanted to see where the Lord might lead us, and, well, I wanted to tell you that I love you."

That was the first time I said those three words to Bethany. I had waited, because I felt the Lord had showed me through Scripture that true love between a man and woman cannot be separated from commitment. It felt hollow to say "I love you" to Bethany without a deeper commitment. So I babbled on awhile about my feelings for her, until I finally asked, "Will you marry me?"

Bethany's mouth dropped wide open. I took out the ring, and she laughed and smiled before finally answering, "Yes, of course." She took off her knitted winter gloves, and I proceeded to put the ring on her wrong hand. We hugged and laughed.

"I think we put it on the wrong hand," she finally said. We laughed more and quickly switched it to the other hand. The walk back to the car felt like a dream. We talked about how perfect the night was, how special it was to see the two blue herons, and how excited we were to get married. As soon as her car door closed, she flipped open her bulky cell phone and called everyone who was important to her.

Over the next four months, Bethany rushed to plan the wedding, while I rushed to plan our honeymoon in Glacier National Park. Before we knew it, we were married, sitting in a cabin, reminiscing about how grateful to God we both were for making all this happen.

Why Do Your Motives for Marriage Matter?

In this section, my goal is to show you the importance of establishing a healthy heart foundation that is equipped to glorify God through your pursuit of marriage.

In chapter 1, we explored the biblical foundation for what it means to glorify God, and then we applied that truth to answer the question "What does it mean to glorify God through your pursuit of marriage?" Our answer was that to glorify God in life, including in our pursuit of marriage, our goal must be to accurately make Jesus known, because through the revelation of Jesus Christ, God is most glorified.

Hopefully, chapter 1 helped ready your mind for Christ-centered dating, but now we need to focus on our hearts. In addition to having the right goal, if we hope to honor the Lord in our dating, we must also have the right motives for marriage.

Imagine if, on the night Bethany and I got engaged, my actions were exactly the same but my motives were completely different. And instead of our love for each other, the night was actually about my own desire to create an Instagram-worthy experience to gain followers! Bethany would have been reduced to a prop in my stage production. Do you see how dramatically the story changes once we attach corrupted motives to my actions? It's no longer about my love for Bethany. Now it's all about me.

"What do you think of that ring, Bethany? It's going to make quite an impression on my Instagram followers, don't you think?" If I had said something like that, the ring probably would have been floating down that creek; or worse, I might have received an imprint of it right between my eyes. Seriously though, would Bethany be pleased with me if I had planned our engagement, not for her benefit, but for the social media impact?

I imagine this is how God feels when we use him to get what we want. Marriage is a gift to us that expresses his love. If this gift becomes more valuable to us than the Giver, we are missing the point of the gift. Do you think it pleases God when our motive in serving him, obeying him, and doing what he wants is so that we can then get the marriage we always wanted?

Do you think God wants a husband looking at him in prayer and then only remembering how wonderful his wife is? Rather, doesn't God want a Christian husband to look at his wife as a reminder of

God's faithfulness and love for him? As Proverbs 19:14 states, "A prudent wife is from the LORD."

If every time a Christian wife prays to God she is only reminded of her greater love for her husband, that is what the Bible calls idolatry. Rather, when a wife feels blessed by her husband, God wants her to remember that everything good is a visible reminder of God's love for her (James 1:16–17).

So our motives for marriage are of the utmost importance if we desire to glorify God.

Why You Want to Get Married Will Guide How You Pursue Marriage

Why do you want to be married? Your answer to that question shapes how you pursue marriage, who you date, who you will eventually marry, and how you will function in marriage one day.

The "want to" is our focus here. Why do you want to be married? To please God, you can't just coldly choose what you know is right for morality's sake. You must want to please God. Going back to my engagement story, it was not enough to do the things I knew would make Bethany happy. I needed to have the right motives. I needed to *want* to please her.

God doesn't want you merely to go through the moral motions of pursuing marriage biblically by following all the right rules. That doesn't make him happy. He wants you to want to please him. Yes, your actions need to be biblical. But these actions must be done with joy in your heart. God wants your desire for a relationship to be married to your desire to please him. So the best way to answer the question "Why do I want to be married?" is "I want to be married to please God."

If you want to be married only to please yourself, you will not glorify God, and you will not have a joyful future marriage. (Note: you can get married without doing it God's way, but without repentance, it will not be a spiritually joyful and glorifying marriage.) As James 4:3 states, "When you ask, you do not receive, because you ask with wrong motives, that you may spend what you get on your pleasures" (NIV).

Marriage is a gift to us that expresses his love. If this gift becomes more valuable to us than the Giver, we are missing the point of the gift.

If you want to be married because you are lonely, due to a lack of connection with God, you will turn the opposite sex into a false god, because your motive is to replace God with a spouse. If your motive is only to get your sexual desires met, you will pursue people who will fulfill those desires, but who lack inner integrity. If you are tired of feeling like a second-class citizen with all your married friends, other singles will feel your desperation to be married and will be scared away from you, because they won't want to feel that pressure you are putting on them. Again, why you want to get married will guide how you pursue marriage. If your motive is anything other than to please God, you will walk down the wrong path.

Your motives are like the trajectory you choose for your journey. They are like your aim before you fire. Motives are your intentions, your inner compass, or the map you have drawn for yourself before you start walking the trail. If you want to please God by glorifying him in your pursuit of marriage, you must take aim at what will properly reflect God in marriage. You won't accidentally arrive in a glorifying marriage one day. If you want to reflect God in a relationship, you must pursue that type of relationship.

If you are sensing a false motive in yourself, don't feel defeated. Later in this chapter, I will show you how to repent of false motives and choose the right motives for marriage. But first, we need to define what motives truly please God in our pursuit of marriage.

So, to recap, the best motive for marriage is to glorify God, which means to reflect God accurately. The best answer to the question "How can I glorify God in my motives for marriage?" is "I must want a relationship that will properly reflect God."

What Motives for Marriage Please God?

To please God, we must glorify God. To glorify God, we must reflect God. Therefore, to please God in our pursuit of marriage, we must aim at a relationship that will reflect God accurately.

It will take eternity to explore the goodness of God. But the Bible shows us characteristics of God that we can reflect in our lives by the power of the Spirit to bring him glory: love, joy, peace, patience, kindness, goodness, faithfulness, gentleness, self-control, to name a few (Gal. 5:22–23). Jesus is also humble, strong, just, merciful, forgiving, gracious, and so much more. To glorify God, we must seek to reflect him and live like Jesus in all these ways.

But these qualities are not dependent on your pursuit of marriage. All Christians—children, singles, married, widows—should seek to glorify God by reflecting his image in these ways. God wants people to reflect these qualities in marriage, but he wants you to reflect these qualities in singleness too.

You won't accidentally arrive in a glorifying marriage one day. If you want to reflect God in a relationship, you must pursue that type of relationship.

So how specifically can marriage reflect God in ways that singleness cannot? What compels us to pursue marriage if we truly want to please God? Yes, singleness has its own unique advantages to pleasing God (see 1 Cor. 7 for more on this), but our goal is to unpack how pursuing marriage can glorify God.

Here are five unique ways marriage brings glory to God. There are other ways, but these are especially important and clear in Scripture.

1. Joyful Marital Companionship

Before God created anything, the Trinity already possessed a perfect relationship—Father, Son, and Holy Spirit. In Genesis, there are multiple references to how God reflected this communal nature in creating humans, such as: "Then God said, 'Let us make man in our image, after our likeness'" (Gen. 1:26).

If God were not Father, Son, and Holy Spirit, he might have said he would make man in "my" likeness. But before anything was created, Father, Son, and Holy Spirit existed together in perfect unity.

As John 1:1 states of Jesus, "In the beginning was the Word, and the Word was with God, and the Word was God."

During the creation account in Genesis 1, every time God made something, he "saw that it was good." But in Genesis 2, when God formed man, something was declared not good: "Then the LORD God said, 'It is not good that the man should be alone; I will make him a helper fit for him'" (Gen. 2:18).

It was not good for man to be alone, because man was made in God's image, and God has never been alone. For Adam to properly reflect God, he needed Eve: "So God created man in his own image, in the image of God he created him; male and female he created them" (Gen. 1:27).

I'm not saying you have to be married to glorify God or that single people do not reflect God's glory. All Christians, including those who are single, are part of the body of Christ for God's glory (Rom. 12:4–5; 1 Pet. 4:10–11). I am saying that marriage reflects God's communal nature in a way not reflected in any other relationship. The relationship between a husband and wife is unique and reflects something unique about God.

Not only does marriage reflect the community within the Godhead, but it also reflects the community God created between himself and his people, the church. As Ephesians 5:31–33 says:

> "Therefore a man shall leave his father and mother and hold fast to his wife, and the two shall become one flesh." This mystery is profound, and I am saying that it refers to Christ and the church. However,

> let each one of you love his wife as himself, and let the wife see that she respects her husband.

When you pursue marriage because you want to have this joyful marital companionship that reflects God's desire for relationships, you please God.

2. Joyful Fulfillment of Your Marriage Role

Another unique privilege that marriage alone provides is the opportunity to reflect God's character through the marriage roles. As we already saw, males and females equally reflect God's image. But since God made men and women different, they reflect God's image differently. This truth carriers over into marriage (Eph. 5:21–33).

Since this book is about how to honor the Lord in your *pursuit* of marriage, I won't unpack the roles of husband and wife. People walk away from reading the Bible (especially Eph. 5:21–33) believing very different things about how husbands and wives should function in marriage. My intent here is not to define those roles but only to point out that those roles do exist.

If you are egalitarian, you will say those roles are the same. If you are complementarian, you will say those roles are different. But all Christians agree that the marriage bond demands that husbands and wives treat each other in specific, unique ways, unlike any other relationship. When you get married, you become a husband or wife, and you gain a husband or wife. This changes your life, and you can only experience it if you get married.

When you pursue marriage so you can fulfill the biblical role of a husband or wife, you please God.

3. Joyful Sexual Expressions of Love

Another unique privilege God has united to marriage is sex. The Bible is clear that God designed sex to be between one husband and one wife (Heb. 13:4). It records numerous instances of people abusing this design, but only to record the facts of history, not to condone the behavior.

First Corinthians 7 suggests a direct link between the call to marriage and the desire to have sex. Not that God wants you to get married only so you can have sex. But if you have a desire for sex, this is a God-given desire and a sign that God wants you to pursue marriage one day.

> The husband should give to his wife her conjugal rights, and likewise the wife to her husband. For the wife does not have authority over her own body, but the husband does. Likewise the husband does not have authority over his own body, but the wife does. Do not deprive one another....
>
> If they cannot exercise self-control, they should marry. For it is better to marry than to burn with passion. (1 Cor. 7:3–5, 9)

When you pursue marriage to express your love for your future spouse through sex, you please God.

4. Joyfully Giving Life to Another with Your Spouse

All life is precious to God. No matter how a child is conceived, that child is a gift from God. Psalm 139:13 applies to every person ever conceived: "For you formed my inward parts; you knitted me together in my mother's womb."

With that said, God's original design for having children was for it to occur out of the overflow of love between a husband and wife. When they were created, the first husband and wife were told to make babies together: "So God created man in his own image, in the image of God he created him; male and female he created them. And God blessed them. And God said to them, 'Be fruitful and multiply and fill the earth'" (Gen. 1:27–28).

Have you ever asked yourself, *If God had a perfect love relationship within the Trinity and was perfectly happy already, why did he make humans?* God did not make us out of emptiness but out of fullness. God created humans, not because he needed something extra to make himself happy, but because he wanted to share the perfection of himself. Love always produces life. God is love, thus it was natural for God to produce other beings to enjoy his perfect love. God wanted to share the goodness of himself with us.

Likewise, I believe God hardwired this trait into marriage. A healthy marriage does not need children to be happy. Married people seek to have children so they can share their happiness with others. The love a husband and wife share for each other overflows into creating new life together.

At least, this is the ideal. Couples have children for all kinds of reasons. But my point is that if you desire to have children, that is a good, God-given desire.

When you pursue marriage because you desire to be a mother or father one day, you please God.

5. Joyfully Sacrificing Yourself for Another for a Lifetime

This is not an exhaustive list of the ways marriage can bring God glory, but if we were to summarize all the reasons marriage glorifies God, the best word to encapsulate them would be *love*.

Yes, love is a command for all Christians. We are all called to love God and love people (Matt. 22:37–40), not just our spouses. But the love between a husband and wife expresses God's love in a unique way, unlike other human relationships (which also reflect God's love in unique ways).

Love is often misunderstood. Some say it is a choice. Some say it is a feeling. The Bible seems to indicate it is both. If you don't have true affection in your heart for God, you don't love God. Just read 1 Corinthians 13 or the book of Psalms. Love is full of affection, not just dutiful obedience. But if you only have warm affection for God and don't truly obey his commands, you don't love God either. As Jesus said, "If you love me, you will keep my commandments" (John 14:15).

Biblical love involves joyfully sacrificing yourself for the one you love. This is the type of love Jesus offered. He died on the cross with affection in his heart for us. Jesus' love is not hollow (emotion but no action), nor is it hard (action but no emotion). His love is joyfully sacrificial. In John 15:13 he said, "Greater love has no one than this, that someone lay down his life for his friends." Love is about sacrificing—doing what's best for another at great cost to oneself. But it is not only about sacrifice. It is about sacrificing for people for whom you have deep affection.

Marriage creates circumstances for the expression of this type of sacrificial love. Godly marriage offers the world a glimpse of God's love for his people: "Now as the church submits to Christ, so also wives should submit in everything to their husbands. Husbands, love your wives, as Christ loved the church and gave himself up for her" (Eph. 5:24–25). Marriage is sacrifice involving great affection. As God commits to never leave his people, a husband and wife are committing to never leave each other (Heb. 13:4–5).

When you pursue marriage to joyfully sacrifice yourself for your spouse in a commitment that is meant to last a lifetime, you please God.

Why Must Your Motive for Marriage Be Joyful?

You may have noticed that I included the word *joyful* in each of the five motives. I did this because I believe you should only pursue these things if you want to.

God's word does not require you to pursue the covenant bond of marriage. It's okay if you don't have these desires in your heart. It just means you don't desire marriage. Marriage is a biblical option for those who want it, not a biblical command for all Christians. Therefore, to pursue marriage in a way that is pleasing to God, you must pursue it because it is your joy to do so.

It does not make God happy for you to pursue marriage out of moral obligation, fear, or coercion. God wants you to pursue this type of relationship only if you are happy to do it. If you are happy to pursue marriage, it makes God happy for you to pursue it. Paul spoke extremely highly of singleness in 1 Corinthians 7, but notice the emphasis he placed on personal desire in choosing to pursue singleness or marriage:

> I wish that all were as I myself am. But each has his own gift from God, one of one kind and one of another....
>
> If anyone thinks that he is not behaving properly toward his betrothed, if his passions are strong, and it has to be, let him do as he wishes: let them marry—it is no sin. (1 Cor. 7:7, 36)

Paul had the gift of singleness, and he enjoyed it so much he wished others could experience what he experienced. But he recognized that not all have the same gift. Some have the gift of marriage. And if you do have that gift, God wants you to pursue it without any regret: "Let him do as he wishes: let them marry—it is no sin." In 1 Corinthians 7:39–40, Paul concluded:

> A wife is bound to her husband as long as he lives. But if her husband dies, she is free to be married to whom she wishes, only in the Lord. Yet in my judgment she is happier if she remains as she is. And I think that I too have the Spirit of God.

Again, Paul felt singleness led to more happiness. But he also understood that God gave other people different gifts. Notice, however, that Paul's decision-making process involved deciding whether singleness or marriage would make you happier.

Marriage is not a job or a duty. Certainly, it requires hard work and commitment. But you don't have to get married. Just as God will not force you to love him, because love can't be forced, he will not coerce you to get married, because that would not reflect the loving nature he possesses. God joyfully sacrifices for us. He loves us because he wants to.

If you want to get married and it would bring you joy to sacrifice for your spouse, then you are pleasing God in your pursuit of marriage.

You Can Choose Your Motive

Perhaps you've been nodding your head in agreement, but you also have a nagging fear: *What can I do about this? I agree these are the right motives for marriage, but what if my motives are wrong?*

When Christians learn about motives, they often start "repenting" of their bad motives by giving up what they wanted. They assume that the way to repent of wanting something for the wrong reason is to give up that desire completely. If you sense you had a bad motive for marriage in the past, you may feel tempted to believe that the only way forward is to give up your desire for marriage completely.

But that is a mistake—an unbiblical solution to sinful motives. Wanting a good thing for a bad reason doesn't negate the goodness of the thing you want. If your motives are the problem, simply change your motives.

Godly marriage offers the world a glimpse of God's love for his people.

This seems to be Jesus' main point in Matthew 6:1–18. In verse 1, Jesus gave his thesis statement: "Beware of practicing your righteousness before other people in order to be seen by them, for then you will have no reward from your Father who is in heaven." In verses 2–4, he warned us not to seek praise by giving to the needy. In verses 5–15, he said not to seek attention by praying publicly. And in verses 16–18, he said not to fast for that reason either.

Jesus did not say to stop giving to the needy, praying, or fasting. He instructed us to do those things with the right motive—to please God: "And your Father who sees in secret will reward you" (Matt. 6:4, 6, 18). Thus, we can change our motives. Jesus would not have instructed us to exchange bad motives for good if we weren't capable of doing so.

The same Jesus said, "Let your light shine before others, so that they may see your good works and give glory to your Father who is in heaven" (Matt. 5:16). The point, in both instances, is about motives. God doesn't reward good deeds meant to draw attention to you (Matt. 6); he rewards those done for his glory (Matt. 5). The idea is not to stop doing good deeds but to make sure your motives are pure.

The same is true when it comes to your motives for marriage. If you have bad motives for marriage, you don't need to stop pursuing marriage any more than you need to stop giving to the needy, praying, or fasting. Instead, you need to forsake your bad motives and pursue the right ones God is giving you through his Spirit.

At the moment of your conversion, God gave you a new heart with new desires (Ezek. 36:26), a new nature (Eph. 4:22–24), and the Holy Spirit (1 Cor. 6:19). But the process of sanctification is the process of learning to choose to live from the new nature God has given you.

Your sin nature still dwells within your body, but it is no longer the true you (Rom. 7:19–20). In Christ, the true you wants to be married for biblical reasons, because God has given you a new nature that wants good things for good reasons: "I have been crucified with Christ. It is no longer I who live, but Christ who lives in me. And the life I now live in the flesh I live by faith in the Son of God, who loved me and gave himself for me" (Gal. 2:20).

So when you feel bad motives for marriage, just confess those sins to God, like you would any other sin. And then repent by choosing the right biblical motives for marriage that God has placed within you by his Spirit. You can do this by focusing your mind on good motives, for you must "be transformed by the renewal of your mind" (Rom. 12:2). Read what the Bible says about marriage, or review the five biblical motives we discussed in this chapter, and then choose to make those your heart's motives. Believe you want marriage for the right reasons because you know you are a new creation with good motives now. Ask God in prayer to help you embrace these biblical motives for marriage and to reject all false motives. Decide, in the power of the Spirit, to make those your motives as you pursue marriage.

Embrace the truth. Since God has made you pure through Christ, your true heart wants marriage for biblical reasons. While your old sin nature wants marriage for bad reasons, the new nature, the true you in Christ, wants marriage for good, biblical reasons. Reject the sin nature and choose to live from the new nature you have in Christ. As Romans 6:11–14 says:

> So you also must consider yourselves dead to sin and alive to God in Christ Jesus.
>
> Let not sin therefore reign in your mortal body, to make you obey its passions. Do not present your members to sin as instruments for unrighteousness, but present yourselves to God as those who have been brought from death to life, and your members to God as instruments for righteousness. For sin will have no dominion over you, since you are not under law but under grace.

Join Your Goal to Glorify God with Your Pursuit of Marriage

Pursuing marriage is pleasing to God. God made marriage. He didn't make it to be a test for your affection to him: "Who will the Christian choose? God or marriage? Tune in next week for another thrilling episode!"

God created you to be the most satisfied when you truly want what he wants. It's certainly moral to say no to yourself when your desires contradict what God is telling you. But the highest expression of a transformed heart is when you can gladly say yes to what God wants because your greatest desire is to please him.

Therefore, when it comes to dating and pursuing marriage, you must ask, "What does God want me to do?" Many Christian singles assume God's desire is the opposite of their desire—if you want to date someone, then God wants you to sacrifice that desire for him. But that's way too simplistic. Your goal is not to sacrifice your desires for God's. Rather, your goal is to align your desires with his.

God made Adam with a genuine need for a woman. He didn't look at Adam and say, "Darn, what did I do wrong? Adam's not okay alone. I'm not enough for him." No, God made Adam to need Eve, and for Eve to need Adam, which is why he said, "It is not good that the man should be alone; I will make him a helper fit for him" (Gen. 2:18).

If you desire to be married one day, God is almost certainly the one who put that desire in your heart. He doesn't want you to idolize marriage or sin in the process of seeking it out. But if you desire marriage, it makes God happy for you to pursue that desire. You must pursue it his way and follow him through the journey, but it is not an either-or proposition between pursuing marriage and pleasing God. If God has called you to marriage, it pleases him for you to pursue this calling he's placed on you.

It pleases God when a Christian man pursues a Christian woman in an honoring way. It pleases God when a Christian woman sees one of his sons and desires to be his wife. We're not the ones who thought of all this. Marriage came out of the heart of God.

For those who are called to marriage, your pursuit to please God is intertwined with your pursuit of marriage, along with all the other things God has called you to do in life (Eph. 2:10). It pleases God when you obey him. If God put a desire on your heart to be married, pursue it joyfully in obedience to him. And when false motives arise, because your sinful nature is battling for control, reject those sinful urges to want marriage for selfish reasons just like you must reject all the sinful urges that come from your flesh.

If God put a desire on your heart to be married, pursue it joyfully in obedience to him.

In summary, if you want to please God through your pursuit of marriage, start by getting your motives right. Your motives for marriage must mirror your larger motive for everything you do in life—to glorify God. As 1 Corinthians 10:31 instructs, "So, whether you eat or drink, or whatever you do, do all to the glory of God."

3

WOUNDS, IDOLS, AND TRUTH

I needed help.

Bethany and I were doing great during our first six months of dating. I was sensing the Lord leading me to marry her, but a major barrier in my heart was starting to mess things up.

Like most dating couples, Bethany and I enjoyed the emotional high at the beginning. But the initial excitement masked issues God was now bringing to the surface. I was putting pressure on Bethany to fulfill me in ways we both knew she could not. For reasons I will explain shortly, I feared being betrayed, through no fault of Bethany's. I found myself questioning her loyalty. I had an illogical apprehension that she would find someone else and leave me.

Intellectually, I knew that Bethany really liked me and was faithful, but in my heart, I felt fear and distrust. I looked for hidden meanings in every word she said and twisted her statements to validate my suspicions. To make myself feel more secure, I wanted her to say the exact right thing at all times. I pressured her to be a perfect person so I could be sure she wouldn't hurt me.

Meanwhile, the pressure I exerted on her in an effort to overcome my insecurity touched her sensitive feelings of not being enough and feeling unworthy to have a godly relationship. When I would put pressure on her to be who I thought I needed her to be, she would withdraw emotionally, because she knew she could never be the person I was asking her to be. When she withdrew, it worsened my fear that perhaps she would leave me or hurt me one day. It was a vicious spiral where we each let our internal wounds antagonize the other's internal wounds. My pain hit her pain, and her pain hit my pain.

Thankfully, neither of us wanted to give up. We both wanted to figure out how to make this relationship work. We had hard conversations that seemed to clear up the issues for a while, but each time something happened that put us right back into that bad spiral again. I wanted to ask Bethany to marry me soon, but I knew I needed to work on this internal issue first. That's when God led me to a Christian counselor who really helped me unpack what was happening.

"So, of all the girls you dated in high school, you never dated any of them for more than one month?" he asked.

It was true. I quickly broke off nearly every relationship I entered into, and the reason was almost always that I felt the girl could not be trusted.

"Do you see the pattern? It's highly unlikely that all those girls showed themselves untrustworthy so quickly. Now you are fearing that Bethany will betray you one day too. Do you see a familiar theme?"

I nodded.

After a moment of silence, he said, "I have a feeling you know why you have this fear of betrayal."

I paused, and then said, "Because of what happened with my dad."

He nodded.

In previous visits, we had talked a lot about my relationship with my father. He was a very good father, always working hard to provide for my sister and me. He helped coach my hockey teams. He spent lots of time with me. He was very supportive. I truly knew he loved me.

But when I was a young boy, my dad had an affair, and my parents got divorced. Eventually, my dad married the woman he had an affair with. Years later, through God's grace, my dad repented and came back to the Lord. And my stepmom became a follower of Christ too.

One of the big factors that led to their spiritual transformation was a major stroke my dad had when I was ten years old. My father had been like Superman to me. Seeing him severely and permanently handicapped with a traumatic brain injury taught me that life is unpredictable. After that, it always seemed something bad was right around the corner.

The growing realization over the years of what had happened between my dad and mom compounded my trauma with my dad's stroke. You don't tell your three-year-old son the gory details of an affair and divorce. As the years went by, however, I pieced things together on my own: "My parents had a dysfunctional marriage. Dad cheated on Mom. They got divorced. Dad had a major stroke. You never know when tragedy will strike, but it's coming."

All this manifested for me in a fear of betrayal. My conviction that tragedy is inevitable, combined with my deep fear of betrayal, gave me an irrational fear that if I truly committed and opened up to a woman, it would end very badly.

"You are putting pressure on Bethany to become your ideal person who always does everything the way you think it should be done—because you fear being betrayed."

"You're right," I responded. "When I was a boy, before I knew about my dad's affair and before he had the stroke, I always felt so safe around him. But when I got older and he had the stroke, and when I put things together about the affair, my whole world got rocked. I assume everyone is going to betray me now, because that's how life is. Bad things happen, you know?"

Having identified the root of the problem, my counselor and I then started working on the solution. In the ensuing months, the Lord allowed my knowledge of his faithfulness to fill my heart. God showed me that only Jesus is "the perfect one"—the one my heart truly needs. Bethany is a wonderful woman who loves God and bears so much faithful fruit for Jesus, but she is not perfect. Only when I became secure in Christ could I move forward with Bethany without asking her to be something she could never be.

That's a very brief summary of the healing process God brought me through before I was ready to marry Bethany. The Lord also brought her through a season of healing, regarding her fear of not being enough and feeling unworthy to have a godly relationship.

In response to our allowing our wounds to antagonize each other's weak spots, God exposed those areas where we needed healing—and he then strengthened us by his grace. While your story will certainly be unique to you, your story also includes pain. None of us get through life unscathed. Bad things really do happen to all of us. Everyone's wounds are different, but we all need healing to keep those wounds from controlling our lives and relationships.

Becoming Aware of Your Wounds

In chapter 2, we learned about the motives we need to glorify God through our pursuit of marriage. Now we need to address how to uncover wounds and idols that may be causing us to pursue or run from marriage in a dysfunctional way.

Motives dictate what we do. For better or worse, they shape every aspect of our relationship journey. Again, why we want to get married guides how we pursue marriage.

If your "why" for getting married revolves around a wound or unhealthy fear, you're giving that wound or fear power to control your actions in relationships. Wounds cause bad motives. When you live from a wound rather than a healthy motive, you allow past pain to control you and impact your relationships. This often leads to projecting your problems onto innocent people.

For example, part of me wanted marriage to make me feel secure and loved, like when I was a kid, my dad was Superman, and the world still made sense. But that motive caused me to look for a perfect person—and I put pressure on Bethany to be my savior. What happened in the past was dictating how I behaved with Bethany. I was projecting fears that had nothing to do with her onto our relationship. If God had not exposed the lies I was believing—and helped me repent of the sins I committed based on those lies—Bethany and I would never have made it.

The real danger with getting hurt is not the initial pain; the real danger emerges from the lies you come to believe because of that pain. All trauma, including relationship trauma, carries the power to alter your beliefs. For example, you may love dogs, but if you get bit by one, you may start seeing dogs in a different way. The trauma caused by a dog bite can affect you mentally and emotionally long after the physical wound is healed. Your relationship with all dogs may change because of one bad experience. The pain we experience through relationship trauma can control us in much the same way.

Satan is not the father of pain, hurt feelings, or betrayal. According to Scripture, Satan is the father of lies (John 8:44). The devil didn't attack Adam and Eve with threats of violence, nor did he try to possess them and take over their bodies. Satan knew the only way to lead the human heart away from God was to confuse it with lies. Adam and Eve took of the tree of the knowledge of good and evil because they started living from a false narrative manufactured by Satan: "Did God actually say …" (Gen. 3:1). He called into question the goodness of God, and when they believed the lie that God was not good, they chose to disobey him.

Likewise, when you believe lies stemming from past hurts, you let them control how you behave in relationships. The trauma I experienced from my parents' divorce and my dad's stroke led me to believe the lies that everyone would betray me and the worst would always happen. Those lies skewed how I saw relationships and prevented me from responding to Bethany's actual behavior and character; instead, I viewed our relationship through the lens of a false narrative.

When you adopt a false narrative, you fit the facts into a preconceived story line. Instead of facts driving the story, the story influences your interpretation of the facts. This is what past wounds and false beliefs can do to your relationships. Rather than seeing what is actually happening between you and another person, you skew the details to fit your false reality.

The real danger with getting hurt is not the initial pain; the real danger emerges from the lies you come to believe because of that pain.

For example, if you believe the false narrative that you can only be truly happy once you meet your future spouse, you will be unhappy in every dating relationship, because you won't yet know if the person you are dating will be your spouse. This unhappiness will prevent you from ever growing enough with someone to get married.

Or let's say you were teased as a kid and now you believe the lie that you are unattractive. This may cause you to withdraw both inwardly and outwardly and assume everyone looks down on you. Then when people don't engage with you because you've withdrawn, you may assume it confirms your suspicion that they look down on you. Instead of evaluating each relationship encounter individually, you fit everything into the false narrative of "People see me as unattractive."

Or perhaps you lost your temper, causing someone you really like to break up with you. Now you never want to date again because you believe the lie that you are dangerous and always hurt the people you care about most. This lie causes you to push people away, because you don't want to hurt them, while you silently struggle with feeling alone.

My point is, we must root out the false motives that control our behavior. When you react out of past pain, rather than acting intentionally out of a pure motive to honor God in a relationship, you will try to use your relationships to solve your perceived problems. There's always an underlying reason. If you find yourself repeatedly doing something you don't want to do, you can help correct this habit by exposing the reason for it. You must reject the lies you've believed if you hope to operate in a healthy way with the opposite sex.

Dating and marriage are not the remedies to the lies you've believed about life and love. At first, human love might feel like the answer to your pain, the medicine your hurting heart needs. You might think that if you could find someone to love and be loved by, then all this internal pain would vanish.

It's easy to pursue love with the hope that it will heal your hurts and fill your emptiness. Rather than loving and being loved for the glory of God, you expect your partner to make you feel better. Love becomes a drug, something to numb the wounds and mask the pain. The problem is that you always need another hit, a bigger dose, until you become addicted to a feeling that actually makes your wound worse, because it causes you to ignore the real issues inside.

When you expect a relationship to save you, you treat relationships like your god.

Unhealed Wounds and False Gods

Your primary source of joy functions as your god. Whatever you worship is what has power over you. You obey whatever you believe has the power to make you happy. When you use human relationships to solve your problems, you turn relationships into your god. In Psalm 16:1–4, David prayed:

> Preserve me, O God, for in you I take refuge.
> I say to the LORD, "You are my Lord;
> I have no good apart from you."
>
> As for the saints in the land, they are the excellent ones,
> in whom is all my delight.
>
> The sorrows of those who run after another god shall multiply.

David's expression of submission to God communicated his belief that God is the true source of good. The Lord was David's true God, because he was his source of joy. This doesn't mean we can't love or find joy in other people. It just means we can't find love and joy in other people *until* we first turn to God as our ultimate source of love and joy. David also expressed his joy in his relationships with other saints. Finally, he expressed the truth that false gods always make your life worse.

If people replace God as the primary source of your joy, those people become your god. People are broken beings who try to use others to solve their own issues. If you make relationships your god, you choose to be ruled by a god that will use and abuse you for its own purposes. Only the one true God will love you unconditionally, not because he needs something from you, but because he has everything to give. He's the only one without sinful desires; therefore, he is the only God worthy to be trusted. We should choose to trust some people out of grace and love, even after they show themselves to be imperfect. But only God deserves our total trust. We are commanded in the Bible to trust God and love people, but nowhere in the Bible are we commanded to trust people. Again, we must choose to trust some people, because we love them and they love us (Prov. 31:11). But since we all sin and fall short of God's glory (Rom. 3:23), no one deserves our total trust except God himself. I'm not trying to diminish the security and love another human can offer, but no human can offer the security and love only God can give.

God never has an ulterior motive. He wants you to worship him because he knows he is the best for you. Notice how these principles played out in Mark 5:24–34:

> And a great crowd followed him and thronged about him. And there was a woman who had had a discharge of blood for twelve years, and who had suffered much under many physicians, and had spent all that she had, and was no better but

> rather grew worse. She had heard the reports about Jesus and came up behind him in the crowd and touched his garment. For she said, "If I touch even his garments, I will be made well." And immediately the flow of blood dried up, and she felt in her body that she was healed of her disease. And Jesus, perceiving in himself that power had gone out from him, immediately turned about in the crowd and said, "Who touched my garments?" And his disciples said to him, "You see the crowd pressing around you, and yet you say, 'Who touched me?'" And he looked around to see who had done it. But the woman, knowing what had happened to her, came in fear and trembling and fell down before him and told him the whole truth. And he said to her, "Daughter, your faith has made you well; go in peace, and be healed of your disease."

The woman's wound caused her to live a lie. According to the law (specifically Lev. 15), her discharge of blood made her unclean. Not only this, anyone who touched her also became unclean. She wasn't supposed to be in the crowd, and she knew it. She had to hide who she was out of fear others would discover the truth. She was pretending to be clean.

Can't we relate? Aren't we all hiding something that makes us feel unclean, unworthy to be fully known by others? And like her who "suffered much under many physicians, and had spent all that she had, and was no better but rather grew worse," haven't we all made our problems worse by turning to others in an unhealthy way, asking them to be our god, instead of turning to Jesus as the only Savior? Of course, we need others at times to help us in life (Gal. 6:1–6), but turning to another human for the security and love only Jesus can give produces more pain, not less.

When this woman touched anyone other than Jesus, they became unclean. But when Jesus touched her, the opposite happened—she became clean. Spiritually speaking, this is what happens when we turn to Christ for healing. Our sins are too great for other people (1 Tim. 2:5). When we turn to each other for the healing only Jesus can provide, we tear each other down and mess each other up even more. But when we are touched by Jesus, our problems are not too much for him. Our impurity does not infect his purity. Rather, his purity takes over (1 Cor. 1:30–31) and is transferred in full to us through faith and by grace (Eph. 2:8–9).

If you want to avoid more damage from turning to relationship idols for your healing—if you want to stop living a lie and pretending you're fine—you must, like this woman, seek Jesus. After she was healed by Jesus, she was able to live in truth.

Identifying the Lies You've Believed

Now that you understand how wounds and idols negatively affect your motivations in relationships, you need to learn to identify these wounds and idols. To do this, you may require the help of a skilled Christian counselor, like I did. But I also want to share four tips from my experience.

1. Identify What Controls Your Behavior

When we worship false gods, we give them control in our lives. If you want to identify your false gods, look at what controls you.

Like puppets dangling by strings, we react reflexively to our false gods. Do you involuntarily lash out in anger when someone disrespects you? Perhaps you are worshipping your social image and people's perception of you. Do you feel depressed and withdraw into yourself when you think about your ex? Perhaps you idolize this past relationship. Do you retreat in fear and anxiety when you sense someone is interested in you? Perhaps you are worshipping the opposite sex. Do you turn to porn when you feel tired or lonely? Perhaps you worship carnal pleasure.

Our actions reveal what is in our hearts (Luke 6:45). Therefore, whatever you are obeying outwardly is revealing what you are worshipping inwardly. This is one reason bearing fruit is so essential for Christians. Our good deeds are evidence that we follow Jesus in our hearts. We can know Jesus is Lord in our lives when we live by his commands (1 John 2:4–5).

If you idolize marriage, everything you think, say, and do will be shaped by your desire to be married. Of course, it is not wrong to think about relationships, hope for marriage, or dream about meeting "the one." But if everything in your life revolves around your desire to be married, you have made yourself a slave to an idol (Rom. 6:16).

So, to identify who (or what) you worship, ask yourself, "Who do I obey?"

2. Identify What Makes You Really Mad

When people are saved, they typically identify their idols and then give them up. This is what happened in Acts 19 when Paul preached in Ephesus. Idols of the false god Artemis were big business in Ephesus, so when people started turning to Christ—and idol sales plummeted—the idol makers and many others were deeply disturbed. They turned on Paul and his companions and created an uproar in the city (Acts 19:26–29).

When people's idols are threatened, riots happen. Just like with the Ephesians, when someone challenges an idol in our lives, we are ready to fight. Specifically, if the thought of never marrying moves you beyond a healthy sadness to anger or rage, it's quite possible you've turned marriage into an idol.

When we worship relationships, we block God's blessing from coming into our lives. God won't bless you with an idol you worship. By letting go of the lie that only another person can make you happy and embracing the truth that God alone can satisfy the deepest longings of your heart, you put yourself in a position to be blessed by God with marriage one day.

3. Identify Whatever Causes You to Experience Emotional Extremes

Jesus is the source of joy. Nothing else comes close. As Psalm 16:11 states, "You make known to me the path of life; in your presence there is fullness of joy; at your right hand are pleasures forevermore." False gods eventually disappoint.

By worshipping people, we raise them to unrealistic heights in our hearts and minds. But everyone we lift up eventually comes down. Then we usually demonize them.

Idolatry is always marked by these extremes. One minute they are the best person you know, and the next they become the worst. You can tell how much you idolized someone by how much you demonize them once they let you down.

God has a better way. When he's the Lord of your life, you don't need to idolize another person or make them your god. This frees you to love them as they really are—in all their humanity.

So, if you want to find your idols, look at what makes you live on the emotional extremes.

4. Identify What You Obsessively Pursue or Obsessively Avoid

If you practically faint at the thought of staying home on a Friday night, because you will miss your chance to mingle with other singles, you are probably worshipping relationships. If you keep running from one relationship to the next, looking for that so-called perfect person, relationships may be your idol.

Other people are just as obsessive about avoiding relationships. When we idolize someone, we give them the power to make us feel loved or unloved. If we are afraid of being unloved, we may end up doing nothing, rather than risking rejection. Being afraid of interacting with the opposite sex is often an indication that we have forfeited too much power to the opposite sex.

If you are ruled by worry when you consider talking to someone you have feelings for, you probably have an idealistic view of that person that is flowing out of your idolization of them.

An obsessive avoidance is often rooted in an overblown belief that the person or thing you are avoiding is all that can make you happy. You avoid it because if it fails you, you know you have nowhere else to turn. Many people avoid relationships because of the fear of rejection.

Another way you can expose idols is by asking yourself, "What do I obsessively chase, or what do I obsessively run away from?"

Rejecting Messages You Received from Your Wounds

Perhaps while reading this chapter you've identified some false beliefs that have been controlling how you pursue (or run from) relationships.

Identifying such issues is only the first step. Understanding what's holding you back is a good start, but it is not the same thing as experiencing healing. Now that you have exposed the lies, bring them to Jesus and reject them by his authority. Let go of the lies and replace them with biblical truth. Here are five steps to guide you through this process.

1. Label the Lie Concisely

It's hard to reject a lie that remains vague and ambiguous. Therefore, you need to have a clear understanding of the false narrative you've embraced. Articulating a false controlling belief is like shining light into the dark places where the nasty lies have been hiding (Eph. 5:11–15).

One way to do this is to label your lie in a concise sentence or two. For example, I believed the lie that:

- my past sin disqualifies me from marrying a godly spouse.
- all men just want sex.
- all women are controlling.
- I'm worthless and unworthy.
- I'm unlovable.
- somewhere out there a perfect person exists who will finally make me happy in life.
- love is not worth the risk of getting hurt again.

Prayerfully ask the Lord to help you expose the lies you've believed. Try to articulate them as concisely as possible. When you see it clearly and put a name on it, you rob it of its power to secretly control you.

2. Confess Your Sins Stemming from This Lie

I recommend confessing two types of sin. First are sins of belief. Embracing unbiblical beliefs is a sin. So, start by confessing to God the unbiblical beliefs you have embraced.

Second are sins of action. When we believe lies, we live in sinful ways. If you've believed that all men just want sex, you may have had lots of premarital sex as a way of trying to feel loved by a man. If you've believed all women are manipulative, you may have acted manipulatively toward women because you felt you needed to trick them before they could trick you. If you've believed you are unlovable because of your past sins, you may have given yourself over to even more sin because you felt it didn't matter. If you've believed the lie that love is not worth the hassle, you may have sinned by living a selfish lifestyle.

Whatever sinful pattern stems from the lie you've believed, confess it to the Lord. He will forgive you (1 John 1:8–10).

3. Verbally Reject the Lie and State the Truth

It helps to verbally reject lies and state the truth. So verbalize that concise summary you created in step 1, and then counteract that lie with what is true. For example, say out loud:

- I reject the lie that I'm unlovable. God will always love me. I'm his child.
- I reject the lie that all men are abusive. Some men are abusive, but God has not run out of godly men.
- I reject the lie that all women are manipulative. Some women are manipulative, but God has not run out of godly women.
- I reject the lie that I'm stupid like I was told. I'm beautifully and wonderfully made because God knit me together in my mother's womb.
- I reject the lie that, if I get married, I will inevitably hurt my family like my dad did. God's grace can break generational trends. I can live differently because the Spirit of the living God is in me.

Proverbs 18:21 says, "The tongue has the power of life and death" (NIV). So say out loud, "I reject the lie that [you fill in the blank]. I believe that [apply biblical truth here]."

4. Memorize a Key Bible Verse

In step 3, I recommended rephrasing biblical truth in your own words. This is a good way of applying the truth to your life and specific situation. But quoting the Bible directly is important too. When Jesus was tempted by Satan, he battled the devil's lies with Scripture: "It is written …" (Luke 4:1–13).

So memorize a relevant Bible verse that counteracts the lies you once believed. These lies may return and try to regain control of you, even after you've rejected them. If that happens, you'll be ready and armed with God's truth. Quote the Bible and then …

5. Keep Moving Forward with the Lord

There comes a point where your introspection must stop. Paralysis by analysis is real. It's important to slow down from time to time to self-evaluate, reject lies, fight back with truth, unpack what happened in the past, and seek the Lord's inner healing.

Once you've done this, however, it's easy to continue going round in circles—to continue the internal analysis without ever moving on. When you do this, you get stuck in the past. Instead of finding freedom from past wounds, you remain in their control.

Once you've identified lies and wounds, confessed your sins, forgiven those who have sinned against you, and believed God's truth instead of these false narratives, it's time to move on. You must stop thinking so much about the past, so you can start moving into

God's plan for your life. Trust God's healing. Accept that the past is no longer controlling you. Keep moving forward in life with the Lord (Rom. 12:21).

Now it's time in our journey together to stop looking back at your past and to start looking ahead to your future.

4

JOYFUL "IN" VERSUS JOYFUL "WITH"

After a season of rebelling against God in high school, I went through a healthy season of repenting, healing, and maturing with the Lord as a young adult. When I looked ahead in life, I began praying about things like my career choice, calling, and relationship status. Should I pursue marriage or a life of singleness? What would be more pleasing to God?

First Corinthians 7 complicated the question for me. Before Bethany and I started dating, that chapter worried me. We will dive into it together, but a quick reading of it can easily get you feeling like marriage may be acceptable, but singleness is the path for those who really love God. As verse 38 states, "So then he who marries his betrothed does well, and he who refrains from marriage will do even better."

That verse landed in my chest with a hard thud, not unlike when I played hockey in high school and a huge defenseman hit me when I wasn't looking, crumbling me onto that cold, hard ice.

My deepest longing was to love God with my whole heart. As I tried to project out the next sixty or so years, I wanted to choose the path that would bring God maximum glory. While serving on Mercy Ships, I had read John Piper's *Don't Waste Your Life*. In my bottom bunk, slowly rocking back and forth with the ship, my heart's deepest longings were crystallized. *Yes, that's it!* I thought. *I don't want to waste my life, so I must choose to bring God maximum glory.*

Serving with like-minded Christians in Liberia, and now armed with this biblical insight, I knew I wanted to choose whatever path would bring God supreme glorification. Given my surface reading of 1 Corinthians 7, it seemed obvious that I should pursue singleness rather than marriage so I could fully serve the Lord.

I knew God would allow me to pursue marriage if I couldn't help myself. But that seemed like settling for a silver medal from God. I wanted to go for gold! Deep down, though, I knew I really wanted a wife one day! I was conflicted.

As a single Christian man, I enjoyed the company of my female friends (especially Bethany), and I could see myself having an even deeper connection with one woman in marriage. I also wanted to be a father and have a family of my own. And when I would read the parts of 1 Corinthians 7 about sexual desires, I felt better suited to pursue marriage rather than singleness.

So, in humility, I decided that God had called me to settle for silver rather than go for gold. Even if singleness were the more glorifying choice, I saw the biblical signs pointing me to pursue marriage, and I accepted that. God had clearly given me a desire to be married, and there was also a woman (Bethany) I wanted to marry. So I took comfort in verse 7: "I wish that all were as I myself am. But each has his own gift from God, one of one kind and one of another."

Don't get me wrong, I wasn't disappointed. I was relieved and happy—even thrilled! While I wanted to choose the path that would bring God more glory, a huge part of me didn't want to sacrifice marriage and choose singleness. I'm confident I would have made the sacrifice if God had called me to, but I would have been extremely disappointed if my desire for marriage was left unquenched. So, yes, I happily "settled" for marriage.

Early on in our marriage, Bethany and I had the normal adjusting phase that most couples go through. When two people live together, even if they love each other deeply, friction will occur. For example, I do the dishes when the sink is full. Bethany does them as soon as one dish gets dirty. It's embarrassing to admit how often we fought over such silly things. Minor issues turned into serious arguments, because we didn't communicate kindly during disagreements. When issues cropped up in our marriage, I remembered how 1 Corinthians 7 said that the anxieties of marriage can draw attention away from one's devotion to the Lord (1 Cor. 7:32–35).

Well, I prayed, *I'm sorry, Lord, for having a divided devotion.*

Not every Christian wrestles with the decision to pursue singleness or marriage. But from talking with countless Christian singles, I know that many do, and that 1 Corinthians 7 is a primary reason. I hope to show you that, back then, I dramatically misinterpreted this important passage. Now I see that, through 1 Corinthians 7, God was trying to teach me how to handle trials and disappointments in life. In my youthfulness, I thought I would be the perfect husband and never mess up so badly that I would hurt my wife. I knew other people had problems in marriage. But not me! I'm me, after all! All that to say, I was disappointed with myself for not being perfect and for not having a perfect marriage.

If you get married, you will experience trials and disappointments too. And if you remain single longer than you want or expect, you will find unwanted trials and disappointments in your singleness. No matter how your relationship journey plays out, disappointment is bound to be part of the story.

So, before moving on to section 2, which focuses on how to seek the one God has for you, we need to be prepared for disappointment. Whether you find yourself in a new relationship or remain single for a while longer, both paths involve seasons of disappointment. Avoiding disappointment is not an option; what can help, however, is learning to deal with disappointment to keep our hearts healthy.

What 1 Corinthians 7 Is Really Teaching Us

While the Bible does seem to indicate that singleness offers an opportunity for devoting oneself completely to the Lord, we need to be aware of the context of Paul's words.

Generally speaking, without consideration of individual personalities and circumstances, Paul seemed to consider singleness a better option than marriage. See verse 38, for example: "So then he who marries his betrothed does well, and he who refrains from marriage will do even better."

But Paul also allowed that singleness was not the best choice for all people in every situation: "For it is better to marry than to burn with passion" (1 Cor. 7:9). The same Paul said "it is better to marry" (verse 9) and "he who refrains from marriage will do even better" (verse 38). He wasn't contradicting himself but giving advice for different contexts. Given individual variables, marriage is often the better option.

Paul considered a person's own desires important in deciding whether they should pursue singleness or marriage: "Let him do as he wishes: let them marry—it is no sin" (verse 36). So marriage is clearly a biblical option for those who desire it. Singleness is not a biblical command, like don't steal, love God, or don't lie. If you want to be married, and you are unhappy about the thought of remaining single, you are biblically free to pursue marriage.

Avoiding disappointment is not an option; what can help, however, is learning to deal with disappointment to keep our hearts healthy.

To summarize, 1 Corinthians 7 does not say that either singleness or marriage is always better. Rather, Paul taught that each person should choose the path that best fits their service to God. We must always glorify God to the maximum no matter what life situation we are in.

It is why Paul told married people to act like they were not married (1 Cor. 7:29)! This instruction is especially confusing since he also gave specific instructions for how married people can act properly as husband and wife (1 Cor. 7:3–5).

When each statement is put in context, however, the apparent contradiction vanishes. Remember, Paul said that, generally speaking, singleness is better than marriage because it allows people to give the Lord their undivided attention. When Paul said that married people should live as though they were not married, he wasn't saying to neglect our spouses. Rather, he meant that married people should devote themselves fully to Christ, just as much as someone who has chosen singleness for that reason. Paul meant that those who are married should *focus on the Lord with all their heart.*

Singleness is best for those who can best serve God in singleness—and marriage is best for those who can best serve God in marriage. Paul's point was not about singleness or marriage. Loving God is the point! God is at the center of 1 Corinthians 7. If you depend on singleness to make you happy, you will be disappointed. If you depend on marriage to make you happy, you will be just as disappointed. God is the only solution because only he will never disappoint you.

God didn't create singleness or marriage to be sources of ultimate happiness. Rather, each is a tool for his glorification. Which tool you use is based on the needs you have. A shovel is not better than a saw unless you need a shovel to accomplish your tasks. Singleness is God's gift to you if you have the need for singleness. Marriage is God's gift to you if you have the need for marriage (1 Cor. 7:7).

All gifts from God, however, have the same specific purpose. They are to be used to serve and glorify him. As 1 Peter 4:10–11 teaches us:

> As each has received a gift, use it to serve one another, as good stewards of God's varied grace: whoever speaks, as one who speaks oracles of God; whoever serves, as one who serves by the strength that God supplies—in order that in everything God may be glorified through Jesus Christ. To him belong glory and dominion forever and ever. Amen.

When we glorify God with the gifts he's granted us, including the gifts of singleness and marriage, we experience maximum joy, because that's what we were designed to do. The psalmist said, "Blessed are those who have learned to acclaim you" (Ps. 89:15 NIV). We are blessed when we learn to glorify God.

This is the mindset to have if you hope to glorify God in your pursuit of marriage. I will offer you biblical and practical steps to help you meet the one God has for you (if you are called to marriage). But along the way, I know you will be disappointed. It won't go the way you want. It will happen faster or slower than you want, or the person you think is the one will reject you, or you will reject someone you really like because there are too many red flags. I don't know exactly what it will be, but it will be something. There's always something.

So I encourage you not to try to find the perfect path. Instead, mature enough in the Lord to where you can keep your heart healthy in him as you travel down imperfect relationship paths.

We need to learn the secret to contentment. Paul can help us here too.

Contentment "With" versus Contentment "In"

I'm writing this chapter at my in-laws' house in Springfield, Illinois. Once every summer, Bethany, Logan (my son, age eight), Noel (my daughter, age six), and I spend a week here. As a creature of habit, I tried to get as much work done on this book as I could when I was back home in the familiarity of my office. But I didn't want to stop working on it for a whole week, so I decided to try to carve out some time while visiting with my in-laws.

Everyone is swimming at a family friend's pool, so I have the house to myself—except for an annoying fly buzzing all over the place. As an introvert, I'm good at focusing deeply on one thing at a time. But I'm also easily distracted, and I'm not good at multitasking. If I'm being completely honest with you, I really want to violently murder this fly right now.

But since this isn't my house, I have no idea where the flyswatter is. I tried to use a magazine, but as I fumbled with the blinds, and as the fly kept escaping my death blows, disappearing into other rooms and then reappearing over my head as soon as I sat down again to write, I'm starting to get worried that I'm just wasting my alone time chasing this fly and everyone is going to come back before I can write what I wanted to write today.

Two days ago, my mother-in-law's friend, whose husband passed away a few years ago, came for a visit. At sixty-three, she has been trying to date again, because she would like to remarry, if it is God's will. As we small-talked, I mentioned that I was writing this book. This prompted her to tell me the struggles she was having finding a Christian man near her age whom she enjoyed and who enjoyed her too. I could hear the disappointment in her voice. From what she shared, she has really tried to meet someone, but for whatever reason, it's just not panning out. My mother-in-law chimed in, "She's really put herself out there."

Perhaps you are expecting me to have offered her some magic words of relationship advice. I didn't. Instead, I listened and attempted to empathize with her, trying to imagine how hard that would be. Sometimes people don't need a tip. Sometimes they just need you to acknowledge that life is disappointing and doesn't go the way you want.

Yesterday, my father-in-law's close friend Charly stopped over with his wife. Charly is eleven years younger than my father-in-law, so when my wife was a child, Charly was like that cool younger uncle who would stop by, have all kinds of fun with the kids, and then leave the house a mess for the parents to clean up later. My wife has told me all kinds of stories of how fun Charly was when she was growing up.

Two weeks ago, Charly had an emergency surgery to remove a golf ball–sized tumor from his brain. He wore a bandana during our visit, because he didn't want the big incision wound on his shaved head to scare the kids. Despite the bandana, you'd never suspect he'd had brain surgery. It was his wife's birthday, so we sang and had ice cream cake.

This morning, before everyone left for the pool, Charly called my father-in-law to share more details about his situation. Just before the birthday party, Charly's doctor had told him and his wife that he probably had around a year and half to live. They hadn't wanted to ruin the evening, so they waited to say anything to the family. When I heard the news, I thought back to our visit. We were all celebrating and telling Charly how amazing he looked, while he and his wife were probably wondering what his next birthday would look like. They're currently getting a second opinion and praying for the best.

Whether it be a fly buzzing around while you're trying to work, reentry into the deep end of the dating pool, or a discouraging prognosis, life involves a full range of challenges—from day-to-day annoyances to life-changing trials.

One problem I have with many churches is they teach singles that longing for something other than God, like a relationship, is a sign of discontentment with God. "Oh, you are sad about being single still? Just be more content in God. He's all you need!"

But this advice is inconsistent with how churches deal with other types of trials. No sensible pastor would tell Charly, "Hey, don't sweat it. Just be content in God. He's all you need." While that's true, it's not helpful advice for someone who is genuinely suffering. Jesus knew he was going to raise Lazarus, but he still wept while his friend was dead (John 11:35).

Singleness is best for those who can best serve God in singleness—and marriage is best for those who can best serve God in marriage.

"Be content in Christ and just focus on God" seems like the right answer for any situation, but when you need a hug, it feels more like a slap to the face. Yes, God is our ultimate joy, but he also gave us other good desires, like for marriage. Is wanting to be married really a sign you are discontent with God? Do you really need to be rebuked for simply being honest about this longing? Absolutely not.

In Philippians 4, Paul described a beautiful, profound balance between finding joy in Christ and not pretending we are fine when we aren't really fine. Whether it be a daily annoyance, a dating disappointment, or cancer, God doesn't expect us to pretend we are happy with every unwanted circumstance. I don't need to love that fly, my mother-in-law's friend doesn't need to be happy about being a widow, and Charly doesn't need to rejoice that he has cancer. God doesn't need us to fake it.

Rather, God wants us to see that life is too fickle to be our main source of joy. Only he can be that everlasting well our hearts need. The whole book of Philippians is about finding joy in Christ regardless of our circumstances (Phil. 1:27; 2:14, 17–18; 3:1, 7–8), but chapter 4 makes this point especially clear:

> Rejoice in the Lord always; again I will say, rejoice. Let your reasonableness be known to everyone. The Lord is at hand; do not be anxious about anything, but in everything by prayer and supplication with thanksgiving let your requests be made known to God. And the peace of God, which surpasses all understanding, will guard your hearts and your minds in Christ Jesus. (Phil. 4:4–7)

The advice to "rejoice always" is dangerous and cruel. The advice to "rejoice in the Lord always" is biblical and beautiful. It's not true that prayer always changes our external circumstances. But it is true that, through prayer, God can always increase our peace in his presence. Whether it's me sitting here with a fly buzzing around my head, a widow wondering how else she can meet someone, or Charly seeking a second opinion, we are called to rejoice in the Lord always.

Even though Paul instructed us to find joy in Christ rather than our circumstances, he also had a healthy anxiety over the well-being of an ill coworker (Phil. 2:25–30). Paul knew that, through Christ, he had all he needed, but he also requested that provisions be made for him by the Philippian church (4:16–20). And although he could find the good in false preachers who preached Christ (1:17–18), he also warned us to stay away from such people (Rom. 16:17–20).

Humans are made in the image of God, and God really cares about the actual circumstances in your life (Matt. 6:8, 32–33). Thus, our pursuit of being authentically human reflections of God, as he originally intended, does not mean we need perfect contentment with our circumstances. We seek perfect contentment in Christ, and thus we can be content in him while we are in any circumstance. But nowhere in the Bible are we told we must enjoy unwanted circumstances.

God doesn't want us to be delusional about bad circumstances. Rather, no matter what we face, he wants us to go through them with him:

> Not that I am speaking of being in need, for I have learned in whatever situation I am to be content. I know how to be brought low, and I know how

> to abound. In any and every circumstance, I have learned the secret of facing plenty and hunger, abundance and need. I can do all things through him who strengthens me. (Phil. 4:11–13)

One word can change the meaning a lot! Notice Paul said he had learned to be content *in* any and every circumstance. If you replaced *in* with the word *with*, it would completely change the meaning, like being told to "rejoice always" rather than "rejoice in the Lord always." We are not told to rejoice with being brought low, nor with abounding. We are not told to rejoice with being hungry, nor with having plenty of food. No, we are told to rejoice *in* these circumstances, because Christ is with us through it all.

You don't need to pretend like you are content with singleness if you are not content with it. You don't need to act like you enjoy showing up to another party alone. You don't need to fake it like you are thrilled to be the third wheel again. But through Christ, you can be content in these unwanted circumstances, because Christ is your ultimate source of joy. This is not an excuse to free-fall into depression. Rather, I'm just telling you not to fake it. Be truly happy in Christ always, as Philippians 4:4 commands, but also be authentic about the desires God has given you.

The advice to "rejoice always" is dangerous and cruel. The advice to "rejoice in the Lord always" is biblical and beautiful.

You should only feel guilty if your desire for something other than God is crowding out your desire for God (1 John 5:21). He wants to walk with you through the pain and pleasure, through the trials and triumphs, and through the wanted and unwanted circumstances. It's okay if you are not happy with your singleness as long as you are still happy in Christ.

If You Want to Be Married, Pursue It Joyfully in Christ

The Christian life can be beautifully summarized by 2 Corinthians 6:10: we are "sorrowful, yet always rejoicing." It's okay if your singleness is unwanted, and thus you have a sorrow in your heart, as long as, within that same heart, you are always rejoicing in Christ.

One day, perfect circumstances and perfect contentment in Christ will collide. But before the time when God makes all things new (Rev. 21:1–5), we can still find contentment in Christ even with unwanted circumstances (Phil. 4:4–13).

No circumstance, no matter how good, can fill your heart's need for God (Ps. 16:2). But God gave humans lesser needs that can be found in God's creation. He said of Adam that it was not good for him to be alone (Gen. 2:18), and this was before sin entered the picture. This means that God created Adam to need a wife and Eve to need a husband.

Adam and Eve were never to let anything take God's place in their lives. Nonetheless, in love, God blessed humans with the opportunity to enjoy expressions of his goodness in his creation. God must always be our ultimate source of joy, but he also made us to desire and enjoy blessings that are not him (1 Tim. 6:17).

All good gifts come from God (James 1:17). Everything good in the world reflects God and should make us want the source of that reflection more. All our pursuits of the gifts should remind us of the Giver of those gifts. So even your desire for a spouse can enhance your desire and pleasure in God. But to desire a spouse is good. To want a spouse is not an expression of your lack of joy in Christ.

As we transition from preparing our hearts (section 1) to pursuing marriage (section 2), spend some time preparing yourself for what's ahead. We don't know what's ahead, but we do know, like Paul, the secret to contentment is not found in outer circumstances but rather in a deep, rich inner connection to Christ:

> In any and every circumstance, I have learned the secret of facing plenty and hunger, abundance and need. I can do all things through him who strengthens me. (Phil. 4:12–13)

Section Two

How to Reflect God's Image as You Seek to Meet "the One"

5

THE ONE?

Our week of visiting Bethany's parents in Illinois came to an end. After a round of hugs and goodbyes, we piled into the truck and headed back to Cleveland. When I pulled out my phone to set up the GPS, it gave me three different route options. Bethany and I looked them over and decided to take I-80 East. It required paying some tolls, but since it was a straight shot, and we were towing our camper, we concluded that would be the easiest way back home.

I'm not sure what happened next. Maybe I selected the wrong route, or maybe my GPS overruled my choice. In any case, our drive home was not a straight shot. I know I didn't have to mindlessly follow the GPS barking commands at me, but by the time I realized it was taking us a different way, it was faster to stay the course rather than return to the original route.

We didn't stay on any one highway for more than forty miles at a time. Constantly switching lanes while towing a camper is not my idea of fun. And I'm grateful for God giving us corn, but I'd rather not see it for endless hours on endless country roads. About seven hours into our eight-hour drive, we finally linked back up with I-80 East—just in time to get off again to use the local highways to get home.

Is this what it's like when we are trying to find "the one"? Will one mistake or wrong choice send us down a series of wrong roads that lead nowhere good? This is not the right way to think about the one you will marry. While I do believe the concept of *the one* is biblical, the idea of there being a single route to your intended destination is not entirely accurate.

A better way to use my driving analogy is to say that any of the three options my GPS presented that morning would have led us home. Yes, one route was quickest and more direct than the others, so my choices still had real consequences. Nonetheless, it was possible to take any of the three routes and still get to where we needed to be.

As I read the Bible, I don't see God micromanaging our decisions, but I do see him controlling the outcome of every decision: "We may throw the dice, but the LORD determines how they fall" (Prov. 16:33 NLT).

In chapters 6–8, we will discuss practical steps Christian singles can take to meet the person God wants them to marry. But first, we need to lay the right theological foundation. When you read the epistles in Scripture, most have theology at the beginning and practical living instructions toward the end. This is because our beliefs dictate how we live our lives. My hope is that this chapter will lay the theological foundation for the practical steps in the next three chapters.

While I believe God will put you with the one you're meant to marry, this is no excuse to be passive. Rather, your faith in God's ability to bring about what he desires must encourage you to live freely and boldly, making active decisions that have real consequences (both good and bad) when it comes to relationships.

Why Do Your Beliefs about the One Even Matter?

Years ago, I was an associate pastor in charge of a small group ministry. At least once a semester, a group's meeting was derailed by a theological debate about God's sovereignty and humanity's free will. Inevitably, one person would be firmly Calvinistic (focusing on God's sovereignty) and another person would be firmly Arminian (focusing on humanity's free will). The rest of the group was usually a hodgepodge of contradicting beliefs from both sides of the debate, because they hadn't yet thought about the topic very deeply.

These types of conversations rarely result in changed minds. Too often, people get overheated and hurt each other's feelings. Sometimes, both sides gain a better understanding of why they believe what they believe. Occasionally, there's an apparent winner of the debate, but rarely does the other person—or anyone else—actually change their mind.

That said, I don't want you to think I'm trying to convince you to adopt a specific view of how God's sovereignty operates in our lives. I respect your beliefs, even if they differ from mine. I do hope, however, that we can come to an understanding of how to pursue marriage while trusting God.

My encouragement to you is to consider how your theological beliefs are impacting your behavior around dating and marriage. Are you being too passive and devaluing the responsibility God expects you to take for your own life? Or are you trying too hard and getting anxious that you will make a mistake, missing the biblical emphasis on God's power to accomplish whatever he wills to accomplish?

Your theology about the one will affect your behavior in dating. My hope is that this theological discussion will motivate you to take wise, proactive steps of faith while also experiencing a sense of peace. You can trust God to bring you the right person while also taking personal responsibility for your own life as God has ordained.

Some tensions may arise, such as "How much should I do, and what should I wait for God to do?" But don't let your questions twist what the Bible *has* revealed. Yes, there is some mystery about God's power and humanity's free will, but there are also a lot of answers.

Our questions are like those about the role of our choices in our salvation. Does God elect us and that's it? Or do we need to willfully choose to receive God's grace?

Those are important questions that are outside the scope of this study. But our answers to those questions and others like them can help or hinder our path forward—erring on the side of either passivity or anxiety. Call yourself a Calvinist or an Arminian, but if your beliefs are hindering you from obeying God's commands, something is off.

Trust and Active Participation

According to Scripture, God is fully sovereign to bring about his will in everything:

> In him we have obtained an inheritance, having been predestined according to the purpose of him

> who works all things according to the counsel of his will, so that we who were the first to hope in Christ might be to the praise of his glory. (Eph. 1:11–12)

It says God works "all things," not "some things," according to the counsel of his will, and who you marry is a part of "all things." God works all things out the way he wants them to be worked out, and that includes our relationships.

All too often, people put relationships in a different box than their theology. Many believe that everything is under God's control, while acting as if certain parts of their lives—like relationships—are solely under their own control.

Alternately, a lot of people believe that, since everything is under God's control, they should just wait on God to bring the right person to them. But we don't tell Christian singles to wait for God to drop a job in their lap; we encourage them to go to school, get qualified, and then actually apply for a job.

Our belief in God's sovereignty must not cause us to live passively, as though God will magically do everything for us. Rather, it must cause us to live boldly, since we believe that God will use our actions to accomplish his will. Our trust that God has a sovereign plan is not an excuse to be passive and fearful that we might do something out of God's will. Our trust in God's sovereignty is the very reason we should feel free to act, because we know his power can use our free choices to bring about what he wills to happen.

In Acts 2:23, Peter proclaimed, "This Jesus, delivered up according to the definite plan and foreknowledge of God, you crucified and killed by the hands of lawless men." God planned the cross, but sinful people freely chose to put Jesus on the cross. Killing Jesus was a sin people chose to do, and God never causes sin (James 1:13). Yet the crucifixion was predestined by God to occur before humans were created (Eph. 1:4).

Proverbs 18:22 states, "He who finds a wife finds a good thing and obtains favor from the LORD." Notice the emphasis on finding a spouse here. But Proverbs 19:14 says, "House and wealth are inherited from fathers, but a prudent wife is from the LORD." Here is an emphasis on God giving you a spouse. Both are true. God requires us to act but always has the final say. You need to walk through open doors, but God will open those doors.

Trust God's ability to bring about his will for your future marriage *through your actions*. There are *so* many more Bible verses that highlight God's power to bring about his will (Gen. 50:20; 1 Chron. 29:11–12; Ps. 115:3; Prov. 16:9; 19:21; John 6:44; Rom. 8:28; 9:18; Eph. 2:10; James 4:15, to name a few). And there are *so* many more Bible verses that highlight your responsibility to take wise actions in your life so you follow God's will (Rom. 12:1, 6; Eph. 5:15–17; Col. 4:2–6; James 2:17; 4:17; 1 Pet. 4:10; 2 Pet. 1:5, 10; Rev. 3:20). Study this topic and apply these truths to your thoughts, fears, and questions about your relationships.

Our trust in God's sovereignty is the very reason we should feel free to act, because we know his power can use our free choices to bring about what he wills to happen.

For now, though, know that you can trust God to lead you to the one through your prayerful actions. This trust in God's plan need not lead you into passivity. When we trust God's power to produce his plan, it emboldens us to take prayerful actions bathed in faith.

That's my little pep talk for why your beliefs about this topic even matter. Now let's define what is meant and not meant by this term *the one*.

Is There Such a Thing as *the One* according to the Bible?

When I refer to *the one*, all I mean is "the person God has planned for you to marry."

I don't believe in the concept of a soul mate, which most people use to mean that each of us has just one other person out there who can "complete us" (cue the *Jerry Maguire* scene). I don't believe there is one person for everyone, because God has planned for some people never to get married and others to marry twice, like when a widow marries again (1 Cor. 7:39). And I certainly don't mean that there is some perfect one out there (Rom. 3:23), meaning that if you find this person, with whom you are completely compatible, you will never fight and always have the perfect marriage together (see chapter 12 for more on this).

I understand why some people are uncomfortable with *the one*, because it's so easy to attach any number of false ideas to it. Older married couples seem especially intent on trying to stomp out the use of this phrase, because they see so many young people misled by it.

After decades of ups and downs in your own marriage, you gain firsthand knowledge that a successful marriage is less about finding a perfect person and more about learning to love a flawed person. The glassy-eyed youths, scampering about the church, fawning over each other with puppy love, scare the older married people. In genuine love and concern, they want to help younger people avoid getting hurt or misled into a bad relationship because they are under the belief that this person with red flags is still the one. And so, like an older dog trying to teach a puppy how to behave, many of them growl in frustration: "Knock it off. There's no such thing as the one. Just pick someone and learn to love them."

While I agree with the heart behind this advice—a successful marriage is less about compatibility and more about committed love—I still believe it's a huge mistake to ignore the truths in Scripture about God's sovereignty. You can teach people to use their brains and utilize Scripture wisely, while still applying sound theology to their relationships. Good theology, rightly applied, always enhances one's ability to follow the concrete commands in the Bible about love and commitment. So rather than get rid of this idea of the one, which I believe is biblical, we need to teach people the biblical truth of the idea.

Perhaps the most common counterargument is the hypothetical situation where God planned for you to marry one person, but you married the wrong person. Not only have you married the wrong person, but you have set off a terrible cosmic chain of events leading to thousands of other people marrying the wrong people too, because you married someone else's one, who will now also need to marry someone else's one, and so on.

While this argument sounds clever, it's built on a false premise that God is unable to accomplish his plan by his power. The argument is effective against the idea of a soul mate (meaning there is one person who completes your soul). But when you want to convey that God has a plan for who you will marry, a silly argument like this can't undercut the inerrancy of all the scriptures pointing to God's sovereign will over everything. God's sovereign plan is not a treasure map you must follow exactly. Rather, God's sovereign plan is his will, which is accomplished through his power.

Again, to be theologically consistent, I believe there is such a thing as the one when what you mean by this phrase is "the person God has planned for you to marry." Perhaps the best example in Scripture is found in Genesis 24:14. Abraham sent his servant to find a wife for his son Isaac. The servant then prayed to the Lord:

> Let the young woman to whom I shall say, "Please let down your jar that I may drink," and who shall say, "Drink, and I will water your camels"—let her be the one whom you have appointed for your servant Isaac. By this I shall know that you have shown steadfast love to my master.

Here we have the phrase "the one" followed by a reference to God's sovereign plan, "you have appointed for your servant Isaac." This passage does not include prescripts for us, but it does provide us with a biblical pattern that is consistent with God's sovereignty. I'm not advocating that you try to re-create God's love story between Isaac and Rebekah. But this is a biblical example of the one being the person God has planned for you to marry.

Also, this story doesn't mean you can create a specific situation and force God on your command to reveal your future spouse, like the servant appeared to do in this example. If you dig into this story, there are other indications that Rebekah was the one for Isaac. For example, all parties expressed a mutual willingness for this marriage to take place (Gen. 24:8, 58, 67). And it was a biblical union between two equally yoked people (verses 3–4).

Likewise, it's unrealistic to expect God to tell you, "That's the one," when you see someone you don't know. I've received many emails over the years from people totally convinced God told them that someone was their future spouse, but then it didn't work out for some reason—thus proving that God did not actually tell them this person was the one, since God would never say something that is not true (Titus 1:2).

As with other big decisions, God reveals his plans for us through teaching us to rightly obey the Bible, through the Spirit's personal leading in our hearts, and through the actual circumstances in our lives. Does God generally reveal what will happen in the future for other parts of your life? If not, why expect him to tell you who you will marry before you get to know them? (I've talked about how to identify the one in much greater detail in my book *The One: How to Know and Trust God's Sovereign Plan for Your Future Marriage*. Also, in section 3, we will look further at how to assess whether God is telling you to be with a specific person.)

Finding the one is not some spiritual vision quest, with baby angels bouncing around the clouds shooting love arrows at you. Don't expect the shekinah glory to envelop someone when you see them standing at the salad bar, as though God will visibly appoint your future spouse to you in a miraculous way without any biblical confirmation.

Rather, "the one" is a phrase that should remind you that God is in control of your relationships and he can be trusted. You can rest in the knowledge that he has a good plan for you, which he will bring about by his power (Phil. 1:6; Jer. 29:11–13).

Three Types of God's Will

Perhaps you still have questions like, "If God has a plan that he always accomplishes, why do people get divorced?" Or, "If God plans who you will marry, why does God put some people in a marriage where abuse occurs?" Or, "If God plans everything, aren't we mindless robots? What's the point of life if God has a plan that always happens regardless of what we do?"

One of the reasons so much confusion occurs around the subject of God's will is that Scripture shows us at least three types of God's will. While we should not expect to fully know the mind of our Creator, a lot of confusion about God's will can be cleared up by rightly identifying which category of God's will something belongs in.

The three general categories Scripture points to when referring to God's will are his sovereign will, prescribed will, and personal will for individuals:

- God's sovereign will is his preordained plan that was established before the beginning of time. This will is unchanging and is completely dependent on the power of God, not the power of humans, although God still uses people's free choices to accomplish his sovereign will (Ps. 115:3; Rom. 9:18; Eph. 1:11).

- God's prescribed will is what he wants you to do morally. This has also been called God's will of command. It's God's will that we obey God's word, but since we are free to sin, it's clear that God gives us choices here. When we disobey God's will in this sense, we sin and thus are not following his will for our lives (Rom. 12:2; 1 Thess. 4:2–8; 5:15–18).
- God's personal will is what I refer to as the morally neutral decisions God wants us to make in life as individuals (Acts 16:6–10; 1 Cor. 10:31; Phil. 4:6; Col. 3:17).

God's sovereign will always happens. God's prescribed will is what God wants you to do morally, but which you can choose not to do. And God's personal will is what God is leading you to do individually when it comes to certain morally neutral decisions.

For example: It would not violate God's sovereign will for you to switch jobs and move to a different city. If it did, he would prevent it. It also would not go against God's prescribed will for you to switch jobs and move to a different city, because the Bible gives no clear command that would prevent this type of choice. However, it is possible that God simply doesn't want you to do this. Perhaps he wants you to stay at your current job because he knows it's a better fit for you, and you will get a promotion, meet your future spouse, or essentially have a better quality of life there. Through the Spirit's impression on your heart, he could tell you not to switch jobs, even though you could still make that choice without sinning.

God's personal will is where we typically spend our emotional energy. The key to following his personal will is to take seriously his sovereign will and prescribed will.

The subject of God's will deserves an entire book unto itself, but I wanted to address it here because it helps answer those common questions that occur about the one. For example, "Why would God allow a Christian to marry an unbeliever and then get divorced later on?" It's not God's prescribed will for a Christian to marry an unbeliever (1 Cor. 7:39; 2 Cor. 6:14). So, in this sense, the Christian is breaking God's will for their life, like Luke said of the Pharisees: "But the Pharisees and lawyers rejected the will of God for themselves, not having been baptized by him" (Luke 7:30 NKJV). They didn't reject God's sovereign will, because that is impossible. Rather, they rejected God's laws, by not doing what he wanted them to do morally.

The Christian who married an unbeliever rejected both God's prescribed will and God's personal will for them. It was morally wrong, because their union went against God's word, and it also transgressed God's personal will for them. God knew it was a bad fit and that this couple would be miserable together—so much so that they would choose to get divorced later. So he was personally telling them not to do this.

God, in his sovereign will, could have prevented their marriage, but instead, he allowed it to happen. Perhaps God gave this person over to their sin so that they would be disciplined by the consequences of their sinful actions (1 Cor. 5:5).

When thinking about God's sovereignty and human sin, it is important to realize that, even though God never causes someone to sin, he is still sovereign over the outcome of sin. There are examples in Scripture where God directs someone's sins, like when David took a census (2 Sam. 24:1) or Judas betrayed Jesus (John 13:27). But God did not cause their sinfulness. They were already going down a sinful road, and God merely directed the outcomes of their sinfulness. There is not one example in Scripture of someone seeking to live righteously and God causing that person to sin so he could accomplish a certain outcome.

God only directs someone's sin for his purpose when people are already willfully choosing to sin. In such instances, God uses their sinfulness for his sovereign purpose. As Joseph said to his brothers, who willfully disobeyed God by sinning against him, "As for you, you meant evil against me, but God meant it for good, to bring it about that many people should be kept alive, as they are today" (Gen. 50:20).

Bad marriages, abuse, and other sinful things that occur in relationships are not a valid argument against God having a plan for your future marriage. Our actions matter. Other people's actions matter. God doesn't cause sin. But the human ability to sin is subordinate to God's sovereign power to choose to produce what he wants through sin.

My goal here is not to answer every question about God's sovereignty and humanity's free will. I'm simply wanting you to know that you don't need to worry about missing God's will for your future marriage if you are following God's word and seeking to walk with the Spirit. Focus on obeying God's prescribed will and personal will, and God will accomplish his sovereign will.

Pursue Marriage Out of Faith in God's Power to Accomplish His Plan

When you know that God can ultimately bring about whatever result he desires, it frees you to follow him to the best of your ability. As Proverbs 16:9 states, "The heart of man plans his way, but the LORD establishes his steps."

It can be confusing when we think about God's personal will and sovereign will for our lives. We want to know what will happen next, but God usually only reveals what is happening right now. When you focus too much on figuring out God's personal will and sovereign will for your life, the anxiety can build until it feels completely overwhelming.

God's prescribed will is very different, though. Unlike his personal will for our lives or his sovereign will over our lives, God has revealed his prescribed will through Scripture. You can read about what God wanted from the beginning, what God wants you to do today, and what God will cause to happen in the future.

Many people email me and say that God is silent toward them, no matter how much they ask him to reveal his will. This shows a misunderstanding of the revelation of God's prescribed will in Scripture. Every time you open your Bible, you are reading God's will for your life. In one sense, God's will is that you follow his word.

But when you follow God's prescribed will—when you apply the Bible to your life and obey it—you will find a lot of clarity about his personal will and sovereign will for your life as well. God's sovereign will, prescribed will, and personal will for your life all intersect and connect. When you make personal life choices that are reflective of the eternal truths found in Scripture, the Lord will sovereignly lead you down the right path he has for you. As Psalm 119:105 says, "Your word is a lamp to my feet and a light to my path."

Through Scripture, you can read about what God wanted from the beginning, what God wants you to do today, and what God will cause to happen in the future.

Whenever life gets too confusing and you start getting stressed that you are missing God's will, take a step back and look for the big picture. When you pursue your ultimate aim in life—to glorify God by exalting Jesus Christ—God helps you know what little steps to take too.

Remember, our goal is to learn how to glorify God through your pursuit of marriage. To do so, you must reflect Jesus through your pursuit of marriage—and Jesus fully trusted the sovereign plan of his Father (Luke 22:42; John 12:27–28).

Let's turn now to how men (chapter 6) and women (chapter 7) can do this in practical ways.

6

PURSUE HER

When Bethany and I were on the Mercy Ships mission and still trying to pretend we were just friends, we watched *Napoleon Dynamite* on her laptop with our group of friends over and over again. Our friends thought the movie was funny, but Bethany and I took it to a totally different level, often quoting lines and imitating the characters to make each other laugh.

In the movie, Napoleon wanted to ask Trisha, a popular girl at his high school, to a dance. So, naturally, Napoleon drew a "beautiful" (it was not beautiful) portrait of her and gave it to her, with the invitation "There's a lot more where this came from if you go to the dance with me. Yours truly, Napoleon Dynamite."

This scene inspired me. Sitting in my cabin alone one night, I drew a stunning (it was not stunning) portrait of Bethany and taped it to her cabin door with the lines "There's a lot more where this came from if you go to the market with me. Yours truly, Mark Ballenger." Obviously, Bethany was putty in my hands as she marveled at my masterpiece.

Perhaps the funniest part of this story, looking back, is how Bethany's roommates responded. Some of them were older ladies who had not seen the movie. The looks on their faces when they associated me as "the guy who drew Bethany *that picture*" were pretty humiliating. But I didn't care. Bethany was laughing because she totally understood the joke, and that's all I cared about.

Napoleon Dynamite may not be everyone's (or anyone's) idea of what a man ought to be, but the fact that he pursued Trisha is commendable. And my giving Bethany the picture I drew was more than an inside joke; it was one way I pursued her.

There are a variety of ways for a man to pursue a woman—draw a picture, send flowers, grow a friendship with her for a while, ask her on a date, talk to her more than he used to. It's up to each guy to decide how to pursue; he should do what makes sense and what is true to his personality.

In this chapter, we'll look at why the man should take steps to pursue the woman, as well as biblical principles to consider about the dance men and women must perform before dating if they hope to be in a relationship one day.

Why the Man Should Pursue the Woman

Although our society has become more sensitive to limiting what people can be and do based on gender, some common expectations of each gender continue to stand the test of time.

After reading countless comments on my YouTube videos and coaching many single women, it has been my experience that even if a woman has progressive views on relationships and gender, she still wants the man to initiate the dating relationship. Perhaps you know lots of women who love to ask men out on dates. But I've never met a woman—inside or outside the church—who prefers to pursue and ask a man out. Most women, even today, feel like the man should do that.

Are these gender expectations based purely in societal norms or Christian tradition? No, I believe God has designed men and women to play different roles in their relationships with each other. By design, men and women still long for this natural role-playing. Keep in mind that I'm talking specifically about dating relationships, so please don't overextend my advice to other parts of life. If we were talking about marriage, the church, or society, we would need to biblically and thoughtfully work through those topics separately.

Two words capture the essence of how a man and woman should seek to glorify God through their pursuit of marriage. For men, that word is *pursue.* For women, that word is *invite.* In this chapter, we'll focus on the men and the word *pursue.*

Now, the Bible does not *directly* say men should pursue women in relationships. Trust me, if there was a go-to verse about men pursuing women, Christian women would make sure passive Christian men knew about it.

Perhaps the closest approximation is Proverbs 18:22: "He who finds a wife finds a good thing and obtains favor from the LORD." However, if we were to interpret this verse as applying to men only, we would have to take every other verse in Proverbs that mentions a man doing something as only applying to men. When a man is called to avoid the adulterous woman in Proverbs 5, isn't this also a call for women to avoid adulterous men too? Or is avoiding adultery only a man's job? I believe Proverbs 18:22 is best interpreted to mean that finding a spouse is good for both men and women.

Rather than a specific verse or a direct prescription, I believe these gender expectations (pursue and invite) come from general principles and patterns in the Bible. And for reasons I will share later on, this is an important distinction to make.

When applying God's word, it's helpful to know if a passage of Scripture is a prescript, a principle, or a pattern.

A *prescript* is a command. It's a clear rule that always applies. For example, Exodus 20:14, "You shall not commit adultery," is a prescript. It is what it is, and it applies to all of us all the time.

I don't believe the Bible provides a clear prescript about a man pursuing a woman.

A *principle* is a truth to be applied wisely to life. Context and unique variables need to be considered when applying a principle. For example, 2 Corinthians 6:14 says we should "not be unequally yoked with unbelievers." But what if a believing spouse is already married to an unbelieving spouse who wants to remain married? Are they unequally yoked? Yes, but the context of marriage changes how we should apply this principle (1 Cor. 7:12–13).

What if we apply the principle from 2 Corinthians 6:14 to dating? Is dating being yoked together with someone? I think it is. It's not a permanent yoke like marriage, but it's a yoke to some degree. So, based on biblical principles, we can say Christians should not date unbelievers, even though there is no verse that directly proscribes this.

Some people are in favor of "missionary dating," a term used for when a believer tries to be a witness to an unbeliever, while dating them. The Bible does say Christians are supposed to be witnesses to unbelievers (Matt. 28:19). And it doesn't specifically say, "Don't date an unbeliever." So, some argue that it's okay to date an unbeliever. But when we consider biblical principles like not being unequally yoked (2 Cor. 6:14), guarding your heart (Prov. 4:23), and avoiding bad company that corrupts good character (1 Cor. 15:33), it seems a wise application to say that Christians should not date unbelievers.

I believe the Bible provides a clear principle about men pursuing women in relationships, as I will show you in a moment.

In addition to prescripts and principles, the Bible also contains patterns. A scriptural pattern is helpful but less authoritative than prescripts and principles. Prescripts have the most authority. Principles also have authority, but we need wisdom to apply them in our context. A pattern is more ambiguous, because discerning how a scriptural pattern applies requires a deep understanding of the culture and time periods in which the text was written.

For example, Paul's confusing instructions about women and head coverings are a lot easier to understand when you are aware of prescripts, principles, and patterns. Paul was trying to teach the Corinthians to have orderly worship. In that context, he said:

> Does not nature itself teach you that if a man wears long hair it is a disgrace for him, but if a woman has long hair, it is her glory? For her hair is given to her for a covering. If anyone is inclined to be contentious, we have no such practice, nor do the churches of God. (1 Cor. 11:14–16)

Paul referred to a pattern ("we have no such practice," meaning men had short hair and women had long hair) that was relevant at the time, but he only used that pattern to help them see the principle that husbands should lead their wives just as Christ leads the church (1 Cor. 11:3). The pattern of hair length no longer applies in our culture. But the principle of husbands leading their wives does.

I believe the Bible provides a helpful pattern to follow on men pursuing women in relationships.

So why should a man pursue a woman? Because we are prescribed to glorify God, and through biblical principles and patterns, we see that God made the man to have the role of leader in the marriage and the woman the role of helper in the marriage.

Note that this is not a teaching on how men and women should function in society. The Bible doesn't teach that women can't be managers, presidents, and CEOs. I believe they should be these things if they have the gifts and feel called to do so. But when a man and woman interact in the context of romance and committed love, God has called husbands to glorify him by reflecting his leadership and wives to glorify him by reflecting the church's need to respond.

Ephesians 5:31–32 says, "'Therefore a man shall leave his father and mother and hold fast to his wife, and the two shall become one flesh.' This mystery is profound, and I am saying that it refers to Christ and the church."

Marriage is meant to glorify God by reflecting his truths (i.e., "it refers to Christ and the church"). To husbands, Ephesians 5:23–25 prescribes:

> For the husband is the head of the wife even as Christ is the head of the church, his body, and is

> himself its Savior. Now as the church submits to Christ, so also wives should submit in everything to their husbands.
>
> Husbands, love your wives, as Christ loved the church and gave himself up for her.

One way Christ loved the church was by sacrificing himself for her. If a husband and wife are supposed to reflect Christ and the church, the man should make the first sacrifice by pursuing her and risking rejection.

Christ loved the church by seeking her out (Luke 19:10). Jesus pursued the disciples (John 15:16). He does the same for us. If a man and woman are supposed to reflect Christ and the church, it makes sense that the man would pursue.

Who loved first—Christ or the church? First John 4:19 says, "We love because he first loved us." Romans 5:8 says, "But God shows his love for us in that while we were still sinners, Christ died for us." If a man is to reflect Christ, he should initiate the love relationship by showing love first.

In Revelation 3:20, Jesus said to his church, "Behold, I stand at the door and knock. If anyone hears my voice and opens the door, I will come in to him and eat with him, and he with me." If a husband and wife represent Christ and the church, it's right that the man pursues the woman. She must still actively participate, just as the church has to open the door to Jesus.

Through the biblical truth that a husband and wife are supposed to reflect Christ and the church, in combination with the principles of Christ being the initiator of our love relationship with him, it seems biblically wise to say that, in dating, the man should be the primary pursuer.

If a husband and wife are supposed to reflect Christ and the church, the man should make the first sacrifice by pursuing the woman and risking rejection.

Keep in mind that Ephesians 5:21–33 is about marriage, not dating. A boyfriend should not lead his girlfriend like a husband leads his wife. It's not the same level of commitment, and thus the woman should not allow a boyfriend that much authority in her life; nor should the man allow the woman that much authority in his life.

But if dating is meant to be a time for a man and woman to decide if they should marry, it seems wise that they both exhibit some ability to fulfill the coming marriage roles.

Would it be a sin for a woman to pursue a man? I don't think so. She would not be breaking a scriptural prescription. But it might be unwise and could lead to sin in the future; a man who needs to be pursued in dating is unlikely to suddenly turn into a great leader in marriage.

A man should pursue a woman in dating because, in my view, this is the best application of the biblical principles about marriage to the context of dating. Additionally, this is the regular and normal pattern we see through Scripture (e.g., Gen. 2:24; 11:29; 24:4; 29:18;

Ruth 4:13). None of these verses are prescriptions that state a man must pursue a woman in relationships. But they do provide us with a solid and consistent biblical pattern that men and women should follow today.

Seek to Live Out the Spirit of the Principle

Now let me balance this out a bit. I've been careful to highlight the lack of prescription in Scripture about a man pursuing a woman, because prescriptions are rigid. When God gives us a clear command in the Bible, it's incredibly simple to know exactly what he wants us to do. Just do exactly what he said. Don't steal, don't murder, don't lust, do pray, do forgive, do believe in Jesus—these commands always apply to all of us in the same way.

But principles are flexible. While their truths remain the same, their application can vary by individual. The Bible has spoken to millions of people over many different time periods and cultures. And yet, no matter our unique situation, the principles in Scripture can always be applied to our lives (Heb. 4:12).

"The man should pursue" is a principle I see in Scripture. Thus, it is a flexible truth Christians can wisely apply to their situations. We must not ignore it. We sin if the Holy Spirit tells us to apply this principle in a certain way and we don't do it. Still, it's unwise for Christians to create a step-by-step dating road map and expect all people to follow it.

Rather than prescribing a rigid formula, I believe it is wiser to encourage men and women to follow the spirit behind relevant biblical principles. So instead of dictating every twist and turn that a man must follow perfectly, it's better to give general instruction like,

"Head north, not south." Or, "Pursue her. Don't be passive." The specific way a man expresses the spirit behind his masculinity as he pursues a woman should be left to him.

When a Christian man and woman are interested in each other, they don't need to stress out about who says what first, who holds the door, or who pays for dinner. Rather, they should both feel that the man reflects God's intended image of a man and the woman God's intended image of a woman.

Since "men should pursue" is not a prescript, it should not be taken as a rigid rule for every relationship. (We will unpack this more in chapter 7.)

This clarification is important, because dogmatic specifics are a bad idea. If you are Gen X or an older Millennial like me, you may remember the book *I Kissed Dating Goodbye*, which argued for a strict courting model to replace dating. The book was well intended, but it ended up hurting a lot of people.

Why? Because it laid out very rigid relationship rules. These rules did a lot of damage because not everyone's situation is the same. Decades later, I still talk to people who are single because they kissed dating goodbye twenty years ago, and they still haven't picked it up again. But they want to be married, and now they are wondering, *Why is God still keeping me single?*

Other people were hurt by this book because it presented a type of law about dating, and some people equated this law with scriptural authority. Instead of being used to help people, the laws in the book were weaponized to shame them. If you were not following these laws, you may have even been accused of sinning. Please, please, don't use my book in that way.

The principles in my book are not laws; seek to follow the spirit behind each principle, as you follow the Holy Spirit's leading in applying his word to your life. Precisely how Christian singles apply the biblical principles and patterns in the Bible can look different from one couple to the next. If we make rigid rules where the Bible does not, we box ourselves in and create unnatural, unnecessary predicaments for others.

Christian singles don't need to be weighed down with a bunch of complicated, specific steps. Rather, through walking in the Spirit and seeking to express a biblical masculinity or femininity, they will be free to interact with each other in the ways God designed them to do.

When a Christian man who is walking with the Lord likes a woman, he will figure out how to pursue her in a way that is true to his personality and to biblical masculinity. When a Christian woman who is walking with the Lord likes a man, she will figure out how to be inviting toward him in a way that is true to her personality and to biblical femininity. Pursuing and inviting are more about your character, attitude, and motives than about actual steps or words.

When your heart is rightly aligned with God, your God-given maleness or femaleness will flow from you and direct the actions you take. As Jesus said in Matthew 12:34, "For out of the abundance of the heart the mouth speaks."

Three Wise Steps a Man Should Take to Pursue a Woman

Okay, now that we're clear about the differences between principles and prescripts, I want to offer some specific ways a man can pursue a woman he is interested in.

1. Pray for Her

By "pray for her," I don't mean "pray to obtain her." While God is the only one who can give you a godly spouse (Prov. 19:14), your first step when you like a woman should not be to ask God to make her your future wife. Rather than asking God for "that one," ask God to lead each of you to the one he has for you. Prayer is less about God learning what we want and more about us learning what God's will is.

Therefore, instead of praying to obtain a woman you are interested in, start by praying for her. Ask God to lead her to the right man, even if it's not you. Ask God to lead you to the right woman, even if it's not her. Ask God to make it clear to both of you whether you should explore the possibility of dating. And ask him for the willingness to accept if this relationship is not in his plan for you two.

When you pray for a woman you like, it properly positions your heart. A godly man wants what is best for all and what is most glorifying to God. He doesn't want what he wants at any cost. As Jesus said, "For even the Son of Man came not to be served but to serve, and to give his life as a ransom for many" (Mark 10:45).

Praying for this woman will help ensure your heart is in a healthy place when you interact with her face to face. It will help you avoid bad motives, such as manipulating her, seeking validation from her, or presenting yourself to her in an inauthentic way. Praying for her will prepare and position your heart to have pure motives toward her.

A woman appreciates a man who is open and honest with her. If you are a man who has her best interests at heart, and you are patiently discerning whether God wants her and you to proceed further, you will be a breath of fresh air.

Sometimes men feel as though women are horrified to learn a man wants to be more than friends, like she will think he has been friends under false pretenses. Perhaps some women do take it this way, but the single women I have known are more attracted to a guy when they know where he stands, rather than the guy who is always sneaky and guarded.

Prayer will help you have a healthy confidence. I'm not talking about worldly ego or pride, but confidence that flows from a godly strength. A man who is secure in the Lord sends out the vibe to the woman he likes: "I want what is best for you, even if it's not me. But I also want to explore the possibility of us being together. Are you interested to learn more with me?"

A woman doesn't want a needy man who is so fragile he will crumble into a million pieces if she rejects him. Rather, a Christian woman is attracted to a man who is confident and secure enough in the Lord to risk rejection, knowing he will be okay either way. She's looking for a man of strength, expressed through emotional stability. She's not looking for a man who needs her to fill him. No, she wants a man who is already whole in the Lord and with whom she can enjoy a mutually satisfying connection focused on God.

Prayer helps you become that type of man. The presence of God will lead and strengthen you through all the twists and turns of relationships. But to enjoy God's presence, you need to seek him in prayer.

2. Relate to Her

This step is often overlooked. A lot of Christian guys see a woman, pray about her, work up the courage to approach her, and start by saying, "Hi, would you like to go on a date with me?"

While the courage is commendable, the approach leaves much to be desired. Christian women can be guarded about relationships. They know they need to protect their hearts, so their default response is no; and when someone is caught off guard, they often resort to their default position. If she doesn't know you, she may not give you a chance.

When you take time to relate to a woman, before fully pursuing her, you can gauge whether God is leading you to pursue her. I've received countless emails and comments on my YouTube videos saying, "I've fallen in love with an unbeliever. What should I do?" My gut response is usually, *Why did you allow yourself to fall in love with an unbeliever in the first place?*

A Christian woman is attracted to a man who is confident and secure enough in the Lord to risk rejection, knowing he will be okay either way.

People get attached to each other by spending time together, having conversations, and participating in meaningful activities together. Making such connections helps people get to know each other. But if you learn this person is not a Christian or not in a mature enough place to date right now, it's best to guard your heart and back off so you don't get too attached to someone who isn't the one.

By relating before fully pursuing, you can discern if the biblical requirements are met that allow a relationship to work (which I will talk more about in chapter 10). If you start pursuing right away, it's more likely you'll get attached to someone you shouldn't.

Relating to a woman before fully pursuing her will help you in a lot of practical ways too. Maybe you had butterflies and fuzzy feelings the first time you chatted in the foyer at church. But sitting next to her at the party, you found it hard to carry on a conversation and realized you don't have a lot in common. If you had pursued her right away, it might have become complicated. After a second conversation, however, you both know there's little basis for going on a date.

Many times, people can avoid dating then breaking up by realizing early on that it isn't a great match. Relating helps you get to know the other person rather than falling in love with the idea of them.

Even with online dating, it's best to slow down to see if both spiritual compatibility and social connectivity are present. If you like a woman's profile picture and immediately invite her to coffee, you can likely expect dead silence in return. Remember, when she doesn't know you, her default is usually no. But if you send her a message, asking her a thoughtful question that relates to something unique in her profile statement, you'll begin to learn more about her. Maybe then you have a few good conversations over the phone. After relating in this way, it's much more likely she will accept your invitation to go on a date, and it's much more likely you might actually enjoy the date.

All that to say, try relating to the woman you like before fully pursuing her. Your feelings may be confirmed that you should pursue her more, or maybe God will show you that pursuing her is not what's best for both of you.

Some people need a long "relating season," forming a real friendship, before dating. That's the route I took, but I was nineteen when I met Bethany, so it made sense for me then. Others may meet someone online and need only a few days of relating before going on a date to learn more.

Walk with the Lord, and do what he's leading you to do (James 1:5). But it's generally wise to wait to fully pursue her until you know you relate well to each other.

3. Pursue Her

When I decided to fully pursue Bethany and risk our friendship for the sake of something more, she was living in Charlotte, North Carolina, with her good friend and housemate, Laura.

One of the reasons Bethany and Laura were such good friends was because they were in very similar places relationally—both single and in the back half of their twenties. They both had plenty of guys pursuing them, but they were both committed to avoid dating someone out of the blue. They both wanted to please the Lord and preferred remaining single to dating the wrong guy. Whenever they were feeling sad, confused, or excited, they prayed together and confided in each other. They were a great help to each other in staying strong to their Christian convictions.

It can be difficult when one friend starts dating while the other remains single. Thankfully Bethany and Laura did not experience that. Right when I asked Bethany to be my girlfriend, Laura was being pursued by Matt.

Matt was younger than Laura, just like I was younger than Bethany, and this helped Bethany feel even more comfortable with dating a younger man. Beyond a few similarities, though, our relationship variables were pretty different.

Bethany and I had served for months together on Mercy Ships, getting to know each other in a unique way that few get to experience. When I went back to Ohio and she to North Carolina, we had been friends for a year. By the time I felt released by God to pursue Bethany, we were aware that we liked each other and excited to start this new season together. Then we began dating long distance.

Laura and Matt, however, met at church through mutual friends. They hadn't known each other long before Matt made it clear he wanted something more with Laura. She really liked him, but she had been hurt in the past and was extremely guarded. She wasn't leading him on or playing games, but she did send mixed signals, due to her own confusion and woundedness. Some days she acted like she wanted to date him. Other days, she distanced herself, feeling things were getting too serious too fast.

Then Matt decided to go for it fully. I'm paraphrasing, but basically he said, "Look, Laura, I know you aren't sure about us yet, but you need me. You need someone who isn't going to be scared off by you. I know you like me. I like you too. Just give me a chance and I'll show you I'm serious about you." They are now married with three children.

I'm not saying that line is going to work for everyone. Some women would hate for a guy to say that to her. It could sound arrogant and prideful for someone to say that … unless it's actually true. And that's my point. As a man, do what is true of your personality and for your situation.

For me, to be true to my personality and needs at that time, I needed to pursue Bethany through a long friendship and a short season of dating. Matt just went for it. Who was right? Both of us, because if you are not breaking a biblical command, there isn't a right or wrong way to pursue a woman. Just do it.

But What If I Fail?

Our greatest fears are often attached to our greatest desires. If you are a man who desires to love a woman in marriage, you probably have some fears about being rejected.

One way to overcome a fear of rejection is to focus on your greatest desire—not to be married, but to glorify God. You want to be married because this is a way God is calling you to glorify him. But don't forget that his glory is your true aim.

When you remember this truth, your fear of rejection will subside. Why? Because you can still glorify God even if a woman rejects you. When your greatest desire is to glorify God, the fear of women and of being rejected will lose its grip on you. You won't need to idolize a woman and ask her to validate you when you already worship your true God and are validated by your heavenly Father. Whatever you give the power to make you feel like a winner, you also give the power to make you feel like a failure. Don't give a woman this power. Winning a woman is not the scale by which your manhood will be judged. God didn't make relationships for that purpose. Give God alone the power to validate you as a man.

Another way to deal with this fear of failure is to realize that rejection is not failure. Neither is dating a woman you end up not marrying. Winning a woman must not be your goal as a man. You don't pass or fail the test of manhood by getting or losing the girl. Our goal as Christian men is to follow God's will for our lives. If a woman you are pursuing rejects you, that is a win, because you have learned she is not the one.

It is far better to have tried and failed than to have failed to try. Passivity is your real enemy, not rejection. So many men get stuck waiting for God to guarantee the outcome before taking action. But God often reveals his will to us through the actions we take. Action leads to revelation. Don't wait for a revelation before taking an action.

God may not give you an answer about a woman until you pursue her. He won't remove the risk from the pursuit. The risk is an essential part of the pleasures and adventures he has for you. Would you really want to live such a safe life? As men, God created us for something more than this unhealthy obsession with safety.

"But I lack the social skills to pursue a woman!"

Many little steps over a long period of time can equal giant leaps forward. If you struggle with social skills, start small. Over time, if you keep at it, you will make huge leaps forward; but you have to take little steps each day. Talk to a woman you don't know. Strike up a conversation with the grocery-store clerk. Go on a blind date set up by a trusted friend.

If a woman you are pursuing rejects you, that is a win, because you have learned she is not the one.

Even if you think you are failing socially, you are actually learning. Sin is a failure for which we need Jesus' salvation. But not doing social things perfectly (whatever that means) is not a failure. It's called maturing.

Adam was sleeping when God made Eve, Boaz was sleeping when Ruth lay at his feet, Rebekah came to the well, Rachel came to the well—it still takes God bringing the woman. But he will use your efforts and tell you what you need to do to receive the woman he wants you to pursue.

You're a man. You have what it takes because of how God made you. God created you to pursue a woman as you seek to reflect Christ's love for the church. As 1 Corinthians 16:13–14 states, "Be watchful, stand firm in the faith, act like men, be strong. Let all that you do be done in love."

7

INVITE HIM

When our mission trip with Mercy Ships ended, and Bethany and I said goodbye, I assumed we would never see each other again.

Among our core group of friends on the ship were Paul (from New Zealand, late twenties, an ER nurse), Victoria (from Virginia, early thirties, going to medical school), and Rachel (from Tennessee, late thirties, a well-established physical therapist). On the ship, we served, had fun, watched movies, and did all the things friends do together. But in real life, this group would never have come together like it did in Liberia. Our seasons of life were too different.

Now that the magic of Liberia was ending, and real life was awaiting, Bethany and I knew that our relationship could become a quickly fading mirage, a snapshot from the past. Mentally and emotionally, I tried to prepare myself for losing Bethany forever.

That's how I used to deal with the fear of getting hurt. It's safer (not better) to assume the worst—that way you're prepared if it happens. I really wanted something more with Bethany, but our age difference and coming separation led me to assume that our connection would fade. Like dropping another Polaroid picture into a shoebox full of mementos, I prepared for our time together to become a memory of something good I had lost. It was easier to assume the worst than to hold on to the slim hope we would stay connected and be something more one day.

Thankfully, Bethany was more optimistic. Don't get me wrong, I did my share of reaching out and trying to stay connected. But Bethany arranged a few key interactions that helped us transition into being something more than friends.

A few months had passed since we all went back to our normal lives. Bethany and I had been emailing a lot, but that was easily passed off as a friend thing. We talked on the phone once a month, again, just enough that we both felt like we were just friends.

But then Bethany asked if she could plan a time for her, Victoria, and Paul to come see me for a few days. So they all met up and drove to meet me in Ohio, where I was working at a Christian summer camp. I didn't read this as Bethany trying to say she was interested in dating me. It felt more like a reunion of good friends. But it did provide Bethany and me an environment to reconnect outside the bubble of Mercy Ships. We had a great time as friends, and it was a huge blessing for us all to see one another.

After that, things continued as usual. We all kept in touch through email. Bethany and I talked more than we did with the other friends, but I was still confused and doubtful about what I could do since we were in different phases of life. I was a freshman in community college and making minimum wage. I hadn't even chosen a major. It felt impossible to pursue a woman like Bethany.

Then, a few months later, Bethany called. She asked if I wanted to go on a white-water rafting trip in West Virginia with Victoria, Rachel, and her. I gladly accepted, scraped enough money together for the trip, and packed up my camping gear.

Again, this seemed like nothing more than a reunion of friends—and that's what it was. But sitting around the campfire one night, it dawned on me that I was the only guy there. This could have easily been a girls-only trip, but Bethany had intentionally invited me. After Victoria and Rachel returned to their tents, Bethany and I kept talking and continued burning through firewood, until we realized it was 3:00 a.m.!

Before writing this chapter, I asked Bethany her thoughts about how a woman can be inviting without pursuing. When these two trips came up, she said, "I tried to create an environment where an encounter could happen."

Bethany is a wise woman. She found a way to give me a chance to pursue her while still allowing me to be the main initiator throughout our relationship. As friends, I showed the most obvious interest by paying her more attention than others in the group. I couldn't help it. I wanted to make her laugh. Once I sensed God leading me to pursue her, I called and shared my feelings for her before asking her how she felt about me. And when we were engaged, I bent my knee and asked her.

But Bethany created the environments for the encounters that helped us transition from friendship into dating. Otherwise, I wouldn't have pursued Bethany when I did. I'm not suggesting this as a pattern for every guy to follow. In my case, our different ages and life seasons were the only reasons I waited to pursue her.

Being a freshman in college, I had doubts about my adequacy to pursue a woman like Bethany. Without her subtle signs of encouragement, it's unlikely I would have pursued her. While your situation probably isn't like ours, every man has doubts about pursuing the woman he likes. It helps when the woman gives him a sliver of hope that, just maybe, she's interested in him too.

If you are a stone wall, sending nothing but signs of indifference, his inner fears may win out, and he may assume he doesn't have a chance with you. Sometimes, though, there's nothing a woman can do to help a man with his self-doubts. Ultimately, a man needs to have an inner validation in the Lord to find the confidence to pursue a woman. It's not a woman's job to embolden a man to such a degree that he is able to act like a man.

Every man wants his love for a woman to be returned. If he doesn't sense that the woman may respond positively, he may not pursue—and rightfully so. We shouldn't expect a man to chase a woman who acts like she doesn't want anything to do with him. God made both men and women to desire love. A man isn't immune to emotional pain. If he feels you aren't open to him, he will be much less likely to take a risk.

In all honesty, the only reason I took a chance with Bethany as early as I did was because she was receptive and inviting to me. Before I fully pursued her, I wanted to be older, to have already graduated college, to have a good job. But I knew that if I waited until my life was perfectly lined up, I risked losing her altogether.

Bethany wasn't just waiting around for me either. She was open to my pursuing her, but she wasn't sure I would. While she wasn't in a relationship when I openly confessed my feelings to her, she had been going on dates with guys who seemed to have potential. So, as soon as I turned twenty, I took my shot before it was too late. It wasn't ideal. I wanted to have more of my ducks in a row. But God had other plans, so I went with it—and thankfully so did Bethany!

There's never a perfect time to start a relationship. Waiting for the perfect time often means missing the imperfect opportunity—sometimes the only opportunity you may have. Usually, the perfect moment never comes. Those who get things done choose to get to work even when there are obstacles. If you wait for a perfectly clear path, you waste your life, because the perfectly clear path is a mirage.

"I tried to create an environment where an encounter could happen."

Bethany never clearly communicated to me that she would say yes if I asked her to be in a relationship—and I'm really glad, because I didn't want to have all the risk removed. What I did need, though, was to believe there was a chance that she could say yes to something more with me. That was the glimmer of hope her actions gave me.

Some women go to the extreme to be inviting toward a man, and in the process, they remove all the risk. Even if they won't admit it, men want an element of risk. It's part of the attraction. The woman who is still a mystery at some level is deeply alluring to a man.

Over a decade of marriage later, I still love unlocking new aspects of Bethany that I didn't know before. One aspect of a deepening love is discovering new things about each other and with each other. So, don't pursue a man, and don't let a man know you will for sure say yes if he asks you. But if you want him to pursue you, give him some hope.

Why a Woman Should Be Inviting toward a Man

In chapter 6, I described the differences between a biblical prescript, principle, and pattern. Just as there is no prescript for a man to pursue a woman but principles and patterns that point in that direction, the same is true of a woman being inviting toward a man.

It's important to emphasize that the Bible has no commands about women being inviting toward men. This should help guard us against establishing rigid rules for how a woman can interact with a single man she is interested in. But the Bible does contain principles and patterns to help a single woman know how to express her femininity and be inviting toward a man.

Being inviting is not really about what you say, who says what first, or how much of your feelings you reveal. Rather, being inviting is about projecting the essence of your femininity to a man. It's about your character, attitude, and motivations.

The reason a woman should be inviting toward a man is because we all are prescribed to glorify God. Through biblical principles and patterns, we discern that God made wives to glorify him as helpers in their relationships, and husbands as the leaders. *When we apply these principles to the dance before dating, it helps a man lead in the pursuit when a woman is inviting.*

God made Adam with a desire to search for his Eve. God brought all living creatures before Adam so he could find "the one." "But for

Adam there was not found a helper fit for him" (Gen. 2:19–20). Then God made Eve and presented her to Adam. God set them up on their first date, but it was Adam who spoke first and made the first move. She went with him, as he held fast to her, and they became "one flesh" (Gen. 2:22–24).

For two people to become one flesh there needs to be mutual participation. Adam was the pursuer and initiator, but Eve responded to his initiating. Her willingness to follow his leadership invited more leadership and initiation.

The phrase "one flesh" refers to more than a sexual experience, but sex is clearly part of what it means. The physical activity of sex expresses spiritual symbolism that brings God glory. To be blunt, a man needs an erection, and the woman must receive the man's erection into her for sex to occur. The woman doesn't enter the man; the man enters the woman. Again, the man is the pursuer, and the woman is the receiver.

Sex itself illustrates the spiritual roles that a love relationship requires. The man's physical role in sex represents his relationship role in their love. And the woman's role in sex represents hers. God created sex to be a physical expression of the husband and wife's love for each other, so it makes sense that there is a correlation between the physical act of sex and the spiritual roles of a husband and wife.

While a wife can certainly be aroused by her husband's physical attributes, it is more often the wife's physical attributes that arouse the husband into a sexual experience. Her body invites his arousal. She is aroused too, but usually more by his pursuit of her than by his mere presence.

All that to say, scriptural principles and patterns, beginning with Adam and Eve, lead us to say the man should do the pursuing while the woman should do the inviting and responding.

As we established in chapter 6, the husband represents Christ in a relationship, and Christ initiates and pursues a relationship with his church. While this principle is about marriage, it makes sense to apply it to dating, so couples can see if they possess the right qualities to perform the biblical roles in marriage together. One way a man can show that he has the qualities to be the leader in the marriage is by being the pursuer when they are single.

Now we need to examine how wives reflect the church. While Christ pursues the church, the church must respond to Christ's pursuit through prayer and by inviting him into our lives. A bride is to be attractive to her husband, just as the bride of Christ should be attractive to him. Christ's love is unconditional, and he loves us no matter what, but the church should return his love, with an invitation to continue loving us, pursuing us, and leading us. His love should be returned with love: "We love because he first loved us" (1 John 4:19).

This is why I suggest single Christian women *not* take the approach "I'm just waiting to be found by the man God has for me." God has not called you to be a mindless follower who just waits for a man to do everything. That's not what Christ requires from his church. He wants us to use our brains and proactively show our love for him through prayer and service to others. As the church responds by inviting Christ to pursue her, so too a woman should be inviting toward a man she has interest in.

If we want to apply marriage principles to the dating season in a wise and appropriate way, we should do so accurately and consistently. It's common for men to be told to pursue, but women are often encouraged to do nothing. That's inconsistent with the symbolism of Christ and the church, because the church actively participates in the relationship. It doesn't make biblical sense for a single woman to just wait to be found by a man.

While the image of Christ and the church is regarding marriage (Eph. 5:21–33), a single man and a single woman can appropriately express its principles in dating, as a way of testing whether they can fulfill the biblical roles in marriage together. A single woman who is inviting can one day be a wife who is inviting. A woman who merely waits for a man to pursue doesn't accurately reflect the spirit of the role that she will be called to fulfill as a wife in marriage one day.

Learning from Ruth and Naomi

Perhaps the best biblical example of these principles can be seen in the pre-marriage relationship between Ruth and Boaz.

Ruth 1 introduces the godly qualities of Ruth. All the men in the family died, but Ruth was so dedicated to her mother-in-law, Naomi, she decided to leave her native land and return to Bethlehem with her. Ruth 2 then introduces the godly qualities of Boaz. In an act of desperation, Ruth searched for a landowner who would let her work for food—and found Boaz. Not only did Boaz show her kindness, but he went far above and beyond what the situation required (Ruth 2:13).

Ruth 2:10 shows that Boaz was the initiator of their relationship: "Then she fell on her face, bowing to the ground, and said to him, 'Why have I found favor in your eyes, that you should take notice of me, since I am a foreigner?'" Ruth later took bold steps to invite Boaz's pursuit, but Boaz made first contact. Ruth 2:11 explains why:

"All that you have done for your mother-in-law since the death of your husband has been fully told to me, and how you left your father and mother and your native land and came to a people that you did not know before."

Boaz knew of Ruth's desirable traits as a godly woman. And Ruth subsequently became aware of Boaz's desirable traits as a godly man. This is a good example. Before either made a move toward marriage, they each confirmed godly qualities in the other (Ruth 1–2).

But there was a major obstacle. Boaz was not first in line to marry Ruth. It's safe to assume this was why he was not pursuing her. In addition, it seems Boaz was much older than Ruth (3:10), so they were not an obvious match.

I relate to their situation. Boaz and Ruth had a strong connection, but there were also barriers that made him hesitant to pursue her—not unlike my and Bethany's story. Women, please know that every man has doubts about the woman he likes. It's his responsibility to overcome those barriers with the Lord and pursue you, even if the barriers remain. But being inviting to him can make all the difference.

In Ruth 3, the older and wiser Naomi instructed Ruth on how to invite Boaz to pursue her (verses 1–5). This is a great reminder to seek out wisdom from older women who have real experience with men. Your single girlfriends may be supportive, but an older married woman knows a lot about men (especially if she's raised boys into being men), and she can help you sort through what's happening and help you make a good decision.

Ruth followed Naomi's advice and lay at Boaz's feet one night, as he slept by the grain pile: "At midnight the man was startled and turned over, and behold, a woman lay at his feet! He said, 'Who are you?' And she answered, 'I am Ruth, your servant. Spread your wings over your servant, for you are a redeemer'" (Ruth 3:8–9).

Notice that Ruth was proactive. She didn't sit at home waiting for Boaz to work up the courage to pursue her. She didn't fast and pray for months that God would give Boaz a dream to pursue her. She did something proactive and clear.

It's not wrong to wonder about a man, to fast and pray, or to hope that he pursues you. But sometimes, it's better to act in a way that changes the equation. If Ruth had not taken this proactive step, Boaz would not have pursued her, which we can see by his statement to her:

> May you be blessed by the LORD, my daughter. You have made this last kindness greater than the first in that you have not gone after young men, whether poor or rich. And now, my daughter, do not fear. I will do for you all that you ask, for all my fellow townsmen know that you are a worthy woman. And now it is true that I am a redeemer. Yet there is a redeemer nearer than I. Remain tonight, and in the morning, if he will redeem you, good; let him do it. But if he is not willing to redeem you, then, as the LORD lives, I will redeem you. Lie down until the morning. (Ruth 3:10–13)

Note Boaz's comment, "You have not gone after young men." This implies that Ruth had "gone after" Boaz. While some interpret this as Ruth pursuing Boaz, I believe it's more accurate to say that Ruth was inviting Boaz to pursue her. From here on, Boaz took all the steps necessary to make their marriage a reality, including talking to the man who had the legal right to pursue her first.

It all started with Ruth inviting Boaz to pursue her, but once she gave him the green light, he didn't hesitate, just as Naomi had predicted: "Wait, my daughter, until you learn how the matter turns out, for the man will not rest but will settle the matter today" (Ruth 3:18). As I read this, I see a little smirk on Naomi's face, as if she were saying, "See? This is how men work, Ruth. Sometimes they just need a little encouragement." As the last verse in Ruth 3, it feels like Naomi's "mic drop" moment.

After Ruth's invitation in chapter 3, Boaz fully pursued marriage with her in chapter 4. Ruth provided the encouragement, and then Boaz took the leadership. She didn't have to keep inviting him to the point that she became the pursuer—just enough that he understood the invitation.

As the church responds by inviting Christ to pursue her, so too a woman should be inviting toward a man she has interest in.

Notice how the marriage was described: "So Boaz took Ruth, and she became his wife. And he went in to her, and the LORD gave her conception, and she bore a son" (Ruth 4:13). Boaz took Ruth, and this relationship role of initiator was then expressed sexually in marriage: "And he went in to her."

And who received the glory because of this? "Then the women said to Naomi, 'Blessed be the LORD, who has not left you this day without a redeemer, and may his name be renowned in Israel!'" (Ruth 4:14).

God was clearly in this. He arranged for it all to happen. Boaz had to pursue Ruth, and Ruth played an active role in getting the relationship started too. But God received all the glory!

Likewise, I want to encourage you, as a single Christian woman, that you are not bound to "just wait to be found." You are called to bring God glory by reflecting his image as a woman. Don't let the man's role of pursuer prevent you from being an active player in the relationship.

Just as a wife is not a mindless passenger on the bus her husband is driving, so a single Christian woman should help the man pursuing her by being inviting.

Three Wise Steps a Woman Should Take When She Likes a Man

1. Pray for Him

Just as a man should pray for the woman he is considering pursuing, a woman should pray for the man she wants to pursue her.

Some ladies know exactly how to invite the guys they'd like to pursue them, and they are confident to do it. But for others, knowing how to invite a man can be more complicated. Whether you feel confident or clueless, always start with prayer. God will confirm good ideas, convict you of bad ideas, and help you discover ideas you wouldn't have thought of on your own.

Praying for the man you like invites God to speak to you about this man, and it also puts you in the right frame of mind for whatever happens next. Praying for the man you have feelings for is a way to protect your own heart. Prayer invites God's will, not yours, to be done, and it empowers you to be more submissive to the Holy Spirit's leading in your life.

Praying for him will protect you from having a selfish motive, because through your prayers you will cultivate a spirit of putting God first. Rather than wanting the man at any cost, through your prayers you will learn to want him only if it would be glorifying to God, good for him, and good for you.

Thus, prayer should focus on discovering what God wants instead of pleading for what you want. Don't pray that God would make "that man" the one for you. Rather, ask God to reveal to you, in the proper time, if that man—or another one—is the one for you. Prayer can help you decide what steps you need to take to determine whether this man is the one. Prayer prepares you to handle whatever God allows next. Whether you end up dating or never speaking at all, through prayer your heart will be prepared to trust God in full submission.

Your prayers will also enhance your sensitivity to the Holy Spirit's leading. When you are familiar with the voice of God, by spending time in prayer, you are able to decipher in real time when you are trusting your feelings, being tempted by Satan, or truly hearing from God.

If you don't pray first, you will be more susceptible to manipulation and other unhealthy relationship behaviors. It's easy to hear what you want when you have not trained yourself, through prayer, to hear what God is actually saying. On the other hand, preparing in prayer can help you identify fears and false warnings that might prevent you from entering a relationship God wants for you.

So no matter what happens next, when you like a man, start with prayer (Phil. 4:6–7).

2. Respond to Him

Because there has been such an emphasis on men pursuing women, Christian women often forget that they need to respond in a clear way to a man's pursuit.

As Song of Solomon 1 says, "Let him kiss me with the kisses of his mouth! … Draw me after you; let us run. The king has brought me into his chambers" (verses 2, 4). Notice that the woman desired the king to initiate, but she was prepared to reflect his interest level. She could have run the other way, but she wouldn't do that because she wanted to be with him.

Some women don't respond to being pursued in a clear enough way for men to understand what they want. When the men stop pursuing them, because the men's efforts weren't reciprocated, the women wonder, *What happened? Why did he stop pursuing me?*

If the man you like shows interest in you, make sure to respond in a way that shows you want him to continue the pursuit.

Of course, be careful not to overdo it and seem desperate. But far more Christian women seem to make the mistake of not responding enough rather than responding too much.

3. Invite Him

While I've been talking about the principle of inviting a man throughout this chapter, now I want to talk about the literal act of inviting him. Whether it be through talking to him more in a group setting, inviting him to attend an event, or arranging for the two of you to participate in a mutual interest, find a way to be inviting toward the man you like.

On a practical level, I really like this approach, because inviting a guy to do something you're already planning to do is a good balance between doing something and not doing too much. When I was asking Bethany about her thoughts for this chapter, she said, "I suggested things that could be just a friend thing, but I also tried to let you know I'm available if you're interested."

Is it wrong for a woman to be a little clearer than Bethany was with me about her feelings? No, absolutely not! If you feel led to be a little bolder and more obvious about your romantic interest in a man, that is not wrong at all. But from a practical viewpoint, inviting a man into something that could be passed off as just two friends being friendly is beneficial, because if the man declines the offer, the two of you can go your separate ways without needless awkwardness.

It's also beneficial to take this approach because it protects you from doing too much and inadvertently emasculating the man. I usually don't recommend a woman directly tell a man she likes him first. I don't recommend that she write him a long letter expressing her feelings about him. I don't recommend this type of thing because it takes away the man's opportunity to pursue and it can make him feel like less of a man. Something about a woman taking the lead in openly expressing her feelings first can back the man into a corner. It can feel like you are forcing him to act—and if he feels forced, he may say no, because he wants to choose to pursue you.

The other danger in this approach is that you might attract a passive guy who will expect you always to take the lead in everything.

Perhaps as a woman you think this is silly and unfair, since you would not feel weak if a man expressed his feelings first. But from a male perspective, all I can say is that a man wants to feel like a man. He wants to feel strong, not weak. Deep inside, men know they were made to be "hunters." He will be drawn toward the woman who encourages his masculine nature to pursue, and he will be repelled by the woman who takes away his opportunity to express his masculinity.

When Bethany and I were friends on the ship, I needed a new hat. I was busy working, but Bethany and our friends were headed to the market. Since she knew I needed a new hat, she bought one for me. She didn't attach a love letter to it. She just handed it to me and said, "Hey, I know you needed a new hat, and I saw this, so I bought it for you." By going out of her way to help me, it showed me that maybe she was thinking about me like I was thinking about her.

There's no exact formula for being inviting toward a man. For some, simply talking to him will be enough to let the man know he should pursue her more. Or maybe a well-timed compliment a few weeks in a row at church will get the point across. Do what's true of your personality. When your heart is right with God, and you are embracing a biblical femininity through the power of the Holy Spirit, you will find the right words and actions (Matt. 12:34).

If the man is interested, he should get the picture and start pursuing the woman who has been inviting him. If he does not start pursuing after she has sent some signs that she wants him to pursue, then she should interpret this as the man not being interested. She should move on and not keep inviting him to pursue her.

While this can sting a bit, it is a lot better than endlessly waiting for a man to pursue you who may never do so. By being a little more proactive through your inviting presence toward him, you not only increase the chances of him pursuing you, but you also decrease the chances of wasting time on a guy who is never going to pursue you.

A Christian woman should not view herself as a passive bystander in her own life. It is biblical for her to do something more than just wait around to be found.

8

MEET YOUR FUTURE SPOUSE LIKE THIS

After Bethany and I got married, we took a trip to Tennessee to visit our friend Rachel, who had just bought a new house. Not long after the initial joyful greetings, it became clear that something was off with Rachel. Normally positive, happy, and full of life, she seemed to be bearing a weight on her shoulders. She gave us a tour of her house, and we ended up in her new finished basement, where to our surprise, we saw a lot of kid toys.

Rachel explained that, since all her friends were married with children, she wanted a fun place for their kids so they would still visit her. Then she opened up about why she was struggling emotionally. Turning forty had hit Rachel hard, especially because she had expected to be married herself and have kids by that age. She was starting to come to terms with the possibility that she might never marry.

That was why Rachel had decided to buy a house. She always imagined she would take that step with her future husband, but after turning forty, she chose to go ahead and do it anyway. She then told us she really wanted to be a mom and was considering adopting children. She felt like God might be leading her to adopt, and she asked for our prayers. We committed to doing that, and later we all went out to dinner and had a great evening together.

Time and distance caused us to lose touch with Rachel for a while following our trip, especially after the arrival of our son, Logan. Bethany emailed and texted her now and then, but I didn't talk to her for a few years. Then one day, out of the blue, we received a postcard. It was a picture of Rachel, a man I didn't recognize, and a young boy, all sitting cross-legged on the floor in jeans, white shirts, and bare feet. Cheesiness aside, they looked like they couldn't be happier.

What happened? Online dating. Rachel is now happily married with two children—one son from her husband's previous marriage and one they had together.

I wanted to share Rachel's experience here because it's a happy ending to a story I hear frequently—a prolonged season of unwanted singleness. Not all singleness is unwanted, and it's not hard for all people. But this book is for those who want to be married, so I am confident many readers can relate to the struggle Rachel felt.

Rachel never imagined being in her forties when she got married, nor marrying a man who had previously been married. She never expected to have a blended family, and she hadn't dreamed as a little girl of meeting her Prince Charming through online dating. But Rachel is happier than ever to be with this man and to have the family she has. It just didn't look like she thought it would, and it didn't happen in the timing she imagined.

Can you relate? Whether you are in your twenties or your seventies, if you get married, you will likely deal with unmet expectations on how you meet the one. It's far more likely that you will meet your future spouse in an unexpected way than in the way you've always dreamed.

If you want to get married, it's normal to think about how you might finally meet the right person. Many Christians imagine locking eyes with someone at church and God telling them both, "That's the one." Maybe there is someone you grew up with and always imagined would marry you. But few people dream of meeting someone through online dating.

I'm not advocating that online dating is for everyone. I'm only using it as one example of how many people have met their spouses in a way they did not expect.

Before we talk about dating in section 3, let's look at potentially harmful advice we hear regularly, and then I want to offer some highly practical advice that might help you meet someone and begin a relationship.

Weird Things Christians Do in Hopes of Meeting "the One"

In this section, I want to review some common poor advice many Christians give to singles that they would not give them in any other sphere of life. In other words, here are some strategies to avoid if you want to be in a relationship sooner rather than later.

1. Just wait on God to bring the right person into your life!

Perhaps the most common advice Christian singles hear is "Just wait on the Lord to bring the right one into your life." While waiting on the Lord is biblical and part of the equation of meeting the one God has for you, refraining from interacting with other humans runs counter to the spirit behind the biblical command to wait on the Lord.

It was David who prayed, "Wait for the LORD; be strong, and let your heart take courage; wait for the LORD!" (Ps. 27:14). Everyone else in Saul's army sat on the sidelines in fear as Goliath taunted them every day. But David gathered the five stones and walked onto the battlefield to sling one right in the forehead of Goliath. David believed God would deliver Goliath into his hands, but he still personally went out to slay the giant and cut off his head. When it was over, he credited God with the victory (1 Sam. 17:45–49).

Was David expressing a lack of faith when he reached into his bag to sling the stone? Obviously not! David waited on the Lord for victory, but he also took action. Why then would we look judgmentally at Christian singles who do proactive things to meet people? It frustrates me when Christian singles are counseled to "not take matters into their own hands" and "just wait on the Lord," because this is a poor application of spiritual truth. Spiritually, yes, wait on God and don't take matters into your hands. But like David, who trusted God, we still must take action in real life! We act as though trusting God must be expressed through zero practical effort and actions. But that's not how David expressed his faith in God, nor is it how anyone else in the Bible did so. Faith without action is dead (James 2:17).

So yes, wait on the Lord. Don't force something that's not in God's timing. Trust God, since without him, nothing good will happen in your life, no matter how hard you try. But don't misapply or overapply the Bible verses that talk about waiting on God. It's restricting, not freeing, when we tell Christian singles they must do nothing more than wait for God to bring the right person into their lives.

I'm not advocating that Christians pray less, trust less, or hope less that God brings the one to them. I'm just advocating that we pay just as much attention to the biblical principles about wisdom and taking action too. Wait on the Lord, but *follow the Lord* too, when it's time to act to meet the one he has for you.

2. When you stop wanting to be married, then God will let you get married.

A lot of people have heard that God will bless them with a spouse when they let go of wanting one—as if wanting a spouse is an idol that needs to be forsaken. This is not biblical thinking.

I agree that relationships can be an idol and that God will not bless people with idols. But it's too simplistic to say that any single person who wants to be married is idolizing marriage. As we talked about in chapter 2, God will not take away the desires he has given us, even if we've let them get out of balance. Rather, God will sanctify those motives so we can want the right things for the right reason—to glorify him.

What about the seeming abundance of personal testimonies from people who say they were blessed with a spouse once they stopped looking or gave up that desire? Perhaps these people had this experience because relationships truly had become an idol to them. But there may also have been a practical reason for this outcome.

Perhaps when people let go of their desire for marriage, they open themselves up to meeting people in new, unexpected ways.

It's restricting, not freeing, when we tell Christian singles they must do nothing more than wait for God to bring the right person into their lives.

Our expectation of how we will meet the one is sometimes our greatest barrier to actually meeting them. When people stop trying to meet someone, they often start living in a freer way and cease limiting themselves to meeting people in the ways they imagine they should.

Expectations can be limiting beliefs in camouflage. When we hope or expect to meet the one in a certain way, we may inadvertently close our eyes to other ways God could bring that person into our lives. While there is nothing immoral about having relationship expectations about how you will meet, date, and marry the one, they often do more damage than good.

Single Christians often feel confident that God has told them when and how they will meet their spouse or who it will be. When things don't play out the way they expect, they become confused. If what you think God said didn't happen, the most likely reason is that you misheard God. Perhaps you were confusing God's voice with your own internal expectations.

Sometimes people have met the one when they stopped trying because they stopped limiting themselves on who they meet and where they meet them. In a way, this is what happened to me when I met Bethany on that mission trip.

A few weeks before I left for Liberia, one of my mom's friends called the house. My mom wasn't home, but her friend was apparently in the mood to talk. She knew I was going to Liberia, and she asked all kinds of questions about my upcoming plans. Toward the end of our conversation, out of nowhere, she said, "Well, you never know what God might do on this trip, Mark. Who knows, you might meet your future wife."

I burst out laughing. Of all the reasons I was going on this trip, finding a spouse was not one of them. I had just graduated high school, and like any high school kid, I had my fair share of heartbreak. God was using that pain to motivate me to pursue him more. That was one of the reasons I wanted to go to Liberia, to get away from distractions like wanting a relationship. So dating was out of the question for me during that point in my life. And for the record, I did stay true to that conviction. Bethany and I only dated once we got back to the States. My time of intentionally not looking for a relationship while on Mercy Ships, so I could repent of idolatry, was truly needed.

Nonetheless, as you know, my mom's friend was prophetic that day. Despite my laughter and dismissive attitude toward her comment, she was right. So, did God allow me to meet my wife on that mission trip because I wasn't looking? Was God waiting for me not to do something so he could do something? Does my own story contradict my warning to you to avoid using "not looking" as a way of finding your spouse?

No, I don't believe I'm being hypocritical, because as I will explain in the next section, I was inadvertently taking proactive steps that God used to naturally lead me to the one he had for me. It wasn't my inactivity that led God to introduce me to my wife. On the contrary, God brought us into each other's lives through my actions. I didn't know I was taking these steps, and I wasn't trying to take these steps. But God certainly had me taking steps that led me to meet my wife.

When Christians stop looking and then meet their future spouse, in my opinion, it wasn't their lack of looking that led God to connect them with their spouse. It was that they finally started living. God brought someone into their lives when they started doing new things.

The mindset of letting go of marriage often allows people to interact with the opposite sex in a more relaxed way than when they were pressing to meet someone. But this can be achieved in a healthier way than sacrificing your desire for marriage altogether. Again, you don't have to let go of a desire to be blessed with that desire.

To say all this in another way, focusing solely on meeting the one is sometimes what prevents you from meeting someone new. Sometimes relationships that are focused on marriage are pressure-filled, and as a result, they never grow past the early stages. Romance is when a man and woman are focused on each other. Friendship, however, is when two people are focused on common interests.

Friendships (focusing on common interests) involve much less pressure than romances (focusing on each other). That's why it's sometimes best when romances develop from friendship—there is less pressure on the relationship early on. But when you start out focusing on each other, you jump right to romance and thus greater pressure.

To make new friends, there have to be common interests that build bridges to and unite new people. First John 1:7 says, "But if we walk in the light, as he is in the light, we have fellowship with one another, and the blood of Jesus his Son cleanses us from all sin." Walking with Christ is a common bond that will unite you with other people who are walking with Christ.

This is the reason so many people have met someone new when they stopped looking and started pursuing other passions in life. When you serve in a ministry, for example, you are around other people who are also passionate about ministry. The common bond gives you a reason to be friends. The friendship allows you to connect over this common bond rather than focusing so much on each other so soon.

Even pursuing a hobby can help you meet new people, because those people like that hobby too. I'm not a chatty person in public, so I rarely strike up conversations with strangers in day-to-day settings. But when I go to the climbing gym, since I enjoy rock climbing, I almost always end up talking with someone new, because we are both doing something we enjoy. If you want to meet someone new, God may be telling you to focus less on meeting the one and more on talking with people who share common passions.

When we hope or expect to meet the one in a certain way, we may inadvertently close our eyes to other ways God could bring that person into our lives.

Ironically, giving up the hope of getting married can be just as idolatrous as being more open-minded and hopeful for marriage. Sometimes we let go of idols because it's the only way we know of coping with the pain of not having them. A balanced, healthy desire for a good thing is a much better sign that you have a healthy relationship with what you desire. Extremes are the soil in which the seeds of idolatry grow. Your idol for marriage can be expressed through an extreme drive toward or an extreme avoidance of the opposite sex.

So just because you have given up your desire for marriage does not mean you are free from the idol of marriage. To be free means you can do what you want. To be a slave means you must do what someone else wants. When you are free in Christ, you will be free to pursue the good desires he's given you without shame or fear.

With that said, I do think it can be helpful at times to fast from dating. But fasting is a temporary sacrifice for a specific reason. If you need to sanctify your motives for marriage, God may lead you to take a break from relationships so you can get your heart right with him. But this is different from giving up the desire for marriage completely. Eventually the fast ends, and you again take steps to be with the person God wants you with.

I also don't recommend giving up marriage for the purpose of getting married because for every person who met their spouse when they stopped looking, there is another one who only found their spouse when they started looking. And in between are plenty of people who remained single no matter what they did.

Paul often expressed his longing to see certain people (Rom. 1:11; 1 Thess. 2:18; 2 Tim. 1:4), but he didn't try to get what he wanted by deciding he no longer wanted to see them. Paul didn't try to use reverse psychology on God: "Maybe if I act like I don't want to see these people, God will then let me see these people."

God knows our hearts, so there's no point in trying to pretend we don't want to be married when we do. All those mental games are unnecessary. Just be honest with God. Repent of idolatry. Don't arrange your whole life around meeting the one. But also, don't crucify a desire that God is raising in your heart.

If God put a desire on your heart to get married, seek to use that desire to bring him glory.

3. You need to be careful you don't let the person you like know that you like them.

One of the most common ways God introduces people to their spouses is through shared communities. But if you have a "secret admirer" mentality, it will hinder you from connecting well with people God is bringing into your life.

Christians often reverse appropriate interactions with people they like romantically and people they don't. Some Christians try to satisfy their craving for romance by dabbling in emotionally promiscuous friendships with the opposite sex. They become good friends with someone they know they would never date. They open up to this person and spend time with them in such a way that it would be easy to assume they do like this person in a romantic way.

I'm not against opposite-sex friendships for Christian singles. I think they are needed and helpful—and a lot of marriages are formed from friendships like this. But Christian singles need to be careful not to lead each other on and use each other in selfish ways. If you will treat this opposite-sex friend differently when you enter a dating relationship with someone else, then you are probably treating this friend in an unhealthy way. Someone is probably being led on in this type of connection.

On the other hand, when Christian singles like someone, they often avoid them, don't talk to them, and stay guarded so that this person never has a chance to get to know them. Instead of treating them like their friends, they are overwhelmed with fear instead. Toward opposite-sex friends they have no romantic interest in, they are talkative, welcoming, and sometimes inadvertently sending the message that they are interested. But when they like someone, they are distant and unwelcoming, because they don't want to make a poor impression. In other words, we often spend time with the singles we don't want a romantic relationship with and avoid the singles we do.

This is an ineffective approach to meeting the one God has for you. Not only do you need to interact with the person you have an interest in, but your close interactions with opposite-sex friends you are not romantically interested in may be keeping other potential matches away.

All in all, you have to learn to have appropriate boundaries when dealing with the opposite sex that help protect your heart and theirs. But boundaries are not meant to be walls. When you want to be closer to someone, open your boundary instead of making it stronger. Do this wisely and slowly. Trust people and open up in a way that is congruent with commitment and the evidence of trustworthiness.

In summary, try to avoid the common mistake of opening up to people you don't like and never opening up to the person you do like.

Three Ways You Can Meet Your Future Spouse

There are essentially three options for you as a Christian single to meet the one God has for you: the random approach, the natural approach, and the intentional approach.

The Random Approach

The random approach is when you make zero effort to meet anyone while simultaneously hoping you connect with an eligible Christian single person. You might pray every night for a godly spouse, but if you are hoping you randomly run into an eligible Christian single person and have great chemistry with them, you are relying on this approach.

There is nothing sinful about the random approach, but you should know this is the least successful path to meeting other Christian singles. Meeting Christian singles in places where you would not naturally expect to meet them is a low-percentage strategy. While there is nothing wrong with praying and hoping that you will meet someone at the gym, the grocery store, the bank, the dog park, or some other random place, this is simply an unlikely event to occur.

It is possible to randomly run into a Christian single person you like and who likes you back. But it is the least likely option you have when it comes to meeting eligible Christian singles.

The Natural Approach

Most Christians who have found a spouse used this approach, even though they may not have been aware of it.

Many people incorrectly assume they used the random option to find their spouses. Many Christian singles assume everyone is finding success using the random option except them. In reality, what often appears to be the random option is actually the natural option, and these two approaches to meeting the one God has for you are very different. The random option is based on luck, while the natural option is based on common interests.

The natural option is when Christian singles go places and get involved in communities where it is normal and predictable to meet other Christian singles. While you should not expect to run into lots of eligible Christian singles your age at the grocery store or at your secular workplace, you are much more likely to do so on a mission trip, at a singles ministry at church, or at a party thrown by one of your Christian friends.

For example, while it might seem random when people meet, date, and marry their future spouse while attending a Christian college, the reality is that this is a very natural outcome. If you go somewhere that has hundreds or thousands of Christian singles right at the age where they are getting ready for marriage, it is statistically a strong likelihood that many will meet, date, and eventually marry their spouse in this type of setting. People may have not enrolled in college to meet their future spouse, but it is very natural when this happens.

Likewise, it is a natural outcome when people meet their future Christian spouse at church, while serving in a ministry, or through a mutual Christian friend. They may have not intentionally done one of these things to meet someone, but the odds of meeting other Christian singles are much better when you go where other Christian singles are.

This is what happened to me. I didn't go to Liberia and serve with Mercy Ships to look for my spouse. But mission trips like these, where you're gone for months at a time, are typically more doable for people without lots of commitments back home. Naturally, more Christian singles than married people serve at a place like Mercy Ships. And when you get hundreds of Christian singles working together on a common goal, it's natural and expected for hearts to connect.

But it wasn't enough for Bethany and me to show up on the ship. We participated in the community. We each had a job on the ship that contributed to the main reason we were there, which was to provide free health care to the people in Liberia. Bethany worked in the operating room as a nurse, and I worked in the kitchen preparing food for the crew and patients. Our positions on the ship were like regular jobs in that we all had off days, and during those days, we had other ministry opportunities we could be involved with off the ship.

This is where Bethany and I really connected. We both served in the Jesus Film ministry. Several of us would take the Land Rovers and drive into small, remote villages outside of Monrovia, the capital of Liberia. When it got dark, we would set up a projector and show *The Jesus Film*. After the film, we made a gospel presentation and offered to pray for people. The crew then divided into prayer groups, and on occasion, Bethany and I would end up in the same group. We spent the evening praying over people together—a beautiful opportunity to connect on a deep level and see each other in action.

These experiences provided chances for Bethany and me to spend more time together. Driving to and from the villages gave us hours to talk. After serving, we had an experience in common. The point is not to re-create the unique story God wrote for us but to understand the principle that, if you hope to connect with someone, you have to interact with other Christian singles in significant ways. Just showing up to church, sitting down, and then leaving won't accomplish much for you. But if you get involved in a community where you naturally interact with other Christian singles, you have a better chance of connecting with someone.

In reality, what happened between Bethany and me is extremely common. The original ship operated by Mercy Ships was even referred to as the "Love Boat" by alumni, because so many of us found our spouses while serving on that ship. While I'm not saying you should go serve with Mercy Ships to find your spouse (although that might not be a bad idea), I am suggesting you live a life where it would be natural for you to connect with someone.

If you spend all your time in secular friend groups, bars, and workplaces, don't expect to naturally meet another Christian single person around your age who you have mutual chemistry with. This might randomly happen, but it's not likely.

You have to be around other Christians if you want to meet a Christian to marry one day. This is why I recommend that Christian singles try the natural approach. But if that doesn't work, you do have one more option.

The Intentional Approach

The intentional approach goes beyond frequenting places where Christian singles are likely to be; it's when you intentionally go there with the *purpose* of making a romantic connection.

Online dating is the most obvious example. You sign up on an online Christian dating app because you want to meet someone to date. A blind date set up by a trusted Christian friend is another example of the intentional approach.

I recommend the natural approach first, because it's generally easier to connect through mutual interests and friendships. It's also easier to assess someone in real life rather than jumping into dating right away. Even so, I want to emphasize that there is absolutely nothing wrong with being more intentional in meeting Christian singles, as long as your motive is to glorify God. There is nothing immoral about online dating or blind dating.

Unfortunately, the pre-dating process has been the victim of a lot of theological misapplication. Christian singles often fear that if they do anything intentional to increase the odds of meeting the one, they will be guilty of taking matters into their own hands and not trusting God enough.

Again, the key is to be biblically consistent in every area of our lives. When we get sick, we pray *and* go to the doctor. When we want to serve God, we pray *and* sign up for a ministry opportunity.

When we need a job, we pray *and* send out résumés. And yet, when it comes to relationships, many Christian singles just pray. Many believe everything must happen randomly or else God is not leading the process.

Try whichever option you feel God telling you to try. Perhaps God is telling you to try the random approach. It may be the least effective approach, but it's not sinful, and perhaps it will work for you. I personally believe the natural approach is the wisest to start with. I have seen it work most often compared to the other two. If you've given the natural approach a legitimate shot and it's not working, try something more intentional like online dating.

I especially recommend the intentional approach if you feel like you are getting older and the pool of available Christian singles is shrinking. Ideally, the older you are the more mature you are, so you won't need as much time in friendship to connect and assess like you needed when you were younger. If I were single and met Bethany today, I would proceed differently than when I was nineteen. I would move a lot faster, because both of us are more mature than we were then.

Another situation where the intentional approach may be best is if you are somewhat isolated geographically. Perhaps you live in a small town or go to a small church, and thus it is more difficult to meet Christian singles. Something like online dating might be a good option. While online dating does have its own issues, which I won't address here, it does at least give you the opportunity to meet people who claim to be Christian and interested in dating. That's a good start if you are isolated, because if you stay isolated, you are for sure going to remain single.

Lastly, if you are a Christian woman who has heard a lot of teachings about the man pursuing, you may feel uneasy about the intentional approach. It may feel like you are doing what the man is supposed to be doing. While I don't believe a woman should pursue a man, I do believe a woman can pursue being in a relationship. Those are two different things.

Using the intentional approach to create opportunities to meet men should not be confused with actually pursuing or leading a specific man. A woman can actively put herself in situations where she is more likely to meet Christian single men while still reflecting the image of God in the way the Lord designed women to do.

Who You Meet Is More Important Than How You Meet

I like our story. I'm happy I met Bethany in Liberia. I hope you like your story once God puts you with the one.

But in all honesty, how you meet your spouse does not determine whether you will have a good marriage together. Bethany and I, like any honest married couple, will tell you we have had difficult times together. We've gotten into horrible arguments, and we've had intimate moments we'll never share with anyone. We've struggled with knowing how to raise our children in the best way, and we've celebrated seeing our children flourish under our care. We've struggled at unhealthy churches, and we've thrived at healthy churches. We've had big financial swings with our careers for the worse and for the better.

Thankfully, Jesus has brought us through all the storms and made us closer as a result. But during those difficult seasons, I never once thought back to how Bethany and I met. Our origin story is fun to remember and tell, but it is not essential to our daily life. Our character development and connection to Christ are what impact our marriage daily.

Knowing what I know today, if you gave me the choice between having the story of meeting Bethany online or the story of meeting someone other than Bethany on a mission trip, I'm choosing Bethany 100 percent of the time. Trust me, it's not that important how you meet. Who you meet is way more important!

As we close this section about meeting someone and move into section 3 about dating a particular person, I encourage you to spend some time asking God what he's leading you to do. I hope I've made clear that Christians should not feel like there is one rigid road that leads to marriage. Follow God. He will guide you (Prov. 3:5–6).

Some of you may close this book and keep doing what you're doing. That's fine, if you are happy with the results you are already getting. But if you want different results, you need to try something different. Others of you will take real steps of faith that will change your life. Be one of those people.

Maybe you are not waiting on God, but God is waiting on you. Perhaps you need to change your thinking and stop waiting for God to finally do what you ask. Perhaps you need to start listening so you can do what God asks of you.

Waiting is helpful when you know you are not ready to date or if there is no one available who has the qualities of a godly spouse. But waiting as a way of finding a spouse just doesn't make sense. Patience, of course. Wisdom, absolutely. But just waiting is not how relationships start.

A relationship requires the participation of two people, so if you are not playing your part in the search, you may never be in a godly marriage. If everyone has the same mindset and thus everyone is waiting for someone else to find them, how will anyone meet anyone? That's the main point of this chapter. If you really want to meet the one God has for you, you must be proactive in that search.

If everyone has the same mindset and thus everyone is waiting for someone else to find them, how will anyone meet anyone?

As long as you are following God, obeying his word, and seeking to glorify him in your relationship desires, there's nothing wrong with being more intentional. And it might be just what you need.

Section Three

How to Connect and Assess as You Decide Who to Marry (or Not Marry)

9

THE GOAL OF DATING IS NOT WHAT YOU THINK

When Bethany and I got married in 2008, I was still a poor college student. Thus, when my dad offered me his 1989 Oldsmobile Cutlass Supreme, I gladly accepted.

Bethany had already been an RN for a few years, so she had a nice SUV and refused to travel in my beater. I can't blame her, as it would get us to our destination only about 75 percent of the time. I called the tow truck so many times that I maxed out my AAA towing credits.

Thankfully, Bethany and I had a generous group of friends and family who blessed us with financial gifts at our wedding. We invested half of what we received in a Roth IRA; the other half we took car shopping.

With around $6,000 to spend, I was looking for a great deal—and pretty naive about car shopping. When I saw a newer model Toyota Corolla listed online at an incredible price, I just knew this was a deal I couldn't pass up.

When we met the seller, things felt weird right away. First, we met him in an empty parking lot behind some random building. At first, he didn't want me to pop the hood. When I did, it was clear the engine had been rebuilt. After pressing him a bit, he admitted that the car had been totaled and now had a salvage title. Then he resisted my taking a test-drive. When I scoffed at his suggestion of buying a car without a test-drive, he relented but insisted he come too.

I admit there were already plenty of reasons for me to walk away, but the price was so low! Thankfully, the rain made it abundantly clear this was a bad idea. As we sat awkwardly at a red light, Bethany blurted, "I think something is leaking on my head."

"Oh, no problem," the man said quickly. "I can patch that up." By the time we made it back, Bethany was soaked. "We'll think it over," I said, as we quickly walked to Bethany's dry SUV.

After that, I stopped looking for crazy deals and found an older but appropriately priced Honda Civic, took it for a test-drive, got the green light from my mechanic, and confirmed that it didn't leak on Bethany's head. Sold!

Imagine, though, that I had not taken time to properly assess that Toyota Corolla and had ignored the red flags, determined to buy it no matter what. I would have been a fool! The goal of car shopping is not to fixate on one car before you even have a chance to evaluate it, but to find the right car for you. This should be the mindset of Christians when they are dating too.

The goal of Christian dating isn't to marry the person you're dating; it's to find the right person God has for you. It's dangerous to be so committed to a boyfriend or girlfriend that you overlook the truth about them and marry a person that only exists in your mind. Dating to marry is a mistake; dating to find clarity about God's will for you as a couple is a much better way.

Was looking at that Corolla without buying it a failure? No, it was a success, because it helped me overcome my infatuation with it. Likewise, dating someone and learning you should not marry them is a success, because you have found clarity that they aren't the one—and then you can both move on.

The goal of Christian dating isn't to marry the person you're dating; it's to find the right person God has for you.

Defining the goal of Christian dating helps you know how to date. The goal of Christian dating is to (1) *connect* with a person and (2) *assess* if you should marry them.

Why Your Goal for Dating Should Not Be Marriage

Dating is a way to seek answers to your questions about a person. Those questions center on whether you would marry this person—and whether they would marry you. Thus, dating is best seen as a season to seek answers to your marriage questions.

The Bible doesn't mention any healthy, long-term, romantic relationship besides marriage. Therefore, it is a mistake to be content having a boyfriend or girlfriend. Dating is meant to be relatively short-lived, because dating must not be the goal.

Many people assume that the goal of Christian dating is to get married. This is unwise, because you then run the risk of putting your blinders on, ignoring red flags, and pressing ahead to accomplish the goal of getting married to the person you are dating.

The goal of Christian dating isn't to marry the person you're dating; it's to find the right person God has for you.

When you view breaking up as a failure, you try to make it work with the person you're dating, even though you have no real future together. Or you only date people you are already confident you would marry—but this means rejecting people before even giving them a chance, and we must admit that our first impressions are often wrong.

It's okay to reject people early on if you have zero interest in them romantically. You don't need to give everyone a chance to date you. But the more people you cut off early on, the more you limit your romantic options. When marriage is your goal for dating, you may be overly guarded toward the opposite sex and thus never allow yourself to get to know people. Yet many men and women feel differently about each other after getting to know each other better.

For example, I have two good friends whose future wives rejected them the first time they asked for a date. In both instances, however, after getting to know each other better, the women changed their minds. Both of these relationships resulted in marriage, and now both married couples have multiple children. This type of thing doesn't happen to everyone, but it does happen. By cutting people off too early, you may be missing out.

If you only get to know people you instantly have strong feelings for, you allow yourself to be guided by infatuation. That's what it's called when you like someone you don't know, and those feelings are based only on what you hope is true of them. You fall in love with an image in your mind rather than an actual person.

The failure mindset promotes an unhealthy perfectionism when it comes to dating. Perfectionists are often passive people, because they avoid doing things when there is a chance of failure. If you believe breaking up with someone is a failure, you may fear dating anyone, because you know failure is a possibility. But if you limit who you date in such an extreme way, you will have difficulty knowing anyone well enough to know if they are the one.

As you can see, it's important to define your goal for Christian dating, because your goal will dictate how you date. I'm suggesting that the goal is not to marry someone but to find answers to your questions. If you learn this person is the one, that is a success. If you learn this person is not the one, that too is a success.

Christian dating is a tool to figure out if God does or does not want you to marry this person.

Connect *and* Assess

To find answers about the future of a relationship, you must do two difficult things simultaneously. You must *connect* with and also *assess* the other person.

If you connect without assessing, you are basically trying to marry the person, which defeats the purpose of dating. But if you assess without connecting, you may never truly get to know the other person, and they will likely feel judged and unloved, leading to an imminent breakup.

So it's important to find a healthy balance of connecting with a person while also assessing them through a biblical lens. The more you connect, the more you must assess. Once you have thoroughly connected and assessed, it's time to either get married or break up.

If you limit who you date in an extreme way, you will have difficulty knowing anyone well enough to know if they are the one.

Ephesians 5:15–17 instructs, "Look carefully then how you walk, not as unwise but as wise, making the best use of the time, because the days are evil. Therefore do not be foolish, but understand what the will of the Lord is." It's not wise to make it your goal to marry the person you are dating. It's also not wise to make it your goal to find flaws in the person you are dating so you won't marry them. Rather, the purpose of Christian dating should be to "understand what the will of the Lord is."

This goal should guide your prayers. If you continually pray that God will let you two get married, you will focus on trying to make marriage happen rather than figuring out if God wants that. Instead of asking God to let you marry the person you are now dating, ask him to reveal the right person for you.

Remember how Jesus taught us to pray: "Your kingdom come, your will be done, on earth as it is in heaven" (Matt. 6:10).

Courting, Dating, and the Hybrid Approach

Let's assume you've met someone you really like, and you then go to your church for advice on how you two should proceed. There are two main camps of advice for Christian singles who like each other: the courting camp and the dating camp.

A while back, I posted something on social media including the words *Christian* and *dating*. Someone quickly commented, "A true Christian won't date at all. A true Christian will only court!" Not everyone is so extreme to say that Christians who date aren't really Christians, but some people are passionate about this issue. So it's good to remember that the words *courting* and *dating* are not even in the Bible.

Rather than pick one camp that's better for everyone, it's wiser to choose the path that makes sense for each individual. From my perspective, that path often involves a combination of principles from both the dating model and the courting model.

What Is Courting?

Courting gained a lot of momentum in American churches because of the book I mentioned earlier, *I Kissed Dating Goodbye*. Like a spark thrown into a dry field, that book lit a fire, and soon everyone was kissing dating goodbye. But the book didn't just warn about the dangers of Christians participating in dating; it advocated for courting instead.

Christian courting has a lot more rules, structure, and expectations compared to Christian dating. It aims to prevent sins that commonly occur in dating. Because dating had resulted in a lot of worldliness and sexual sin among Christians, when *I Kissed Dating Goodbye* was released, it resonated with a lot of people. It gave them a concrete way to protect themselves and others from getting hurt and falling into sexual sin.

But the extra rules in courting create time-consuming hoops for people to jump through, preventing a strong connection from growing early on in the relationship. This approach is intentional, as courting is meant to keep two people from connecting to each other too quickly or easily. It also prevents issues that can occur when people rush a relationship, but in many cases, it prevents relationships from forming at all. With Christian dating, a man and woman who don't know each other well can go on a few dates to see if there might be potential in the relationship. In Christian courting, this is forbidden.

Christian courting is reserved for those Christians deemed mature enough to be married. You would not court in high school, for example, because you would not get married in high school. When you court, you are saying you are ready for marriage. Not only that, but you are saying you have a strong belief you would like to be married to the person you are courting.

Courting is a short but intense season to see if marriage should occur. Christian courting emphasizes a pre-courting phase that values friendship and group activities before any type of romantic interest is expressed. Before you start courting, you should already have a good idea of who the other person is and whether you could see yourself marrying them in the near future. This requires a long season of friendship to get to know the person before courting.

When a man and woman who are friends want to take the next step in their relationship, the man is expected to do all the relational heavy lifting. Before even talking to the woman about his feelings or asking her out, he first speaks with her dad or another male Christian leader in her life. After getting permission, he then approaches the woman and explains his intentions to court her with the purpose of seeing if marriage is right for them.

A courting relationship is front-loaded, meaning people confess a lot of strong feelings at the beginning of their courting. By contrast, a dating relationship starts with low commitment and then builds. In courting, marriage is discussed on day one, and both are fully aware of their specific intention of seeing if marriage is appropriate for them. During the friendship phase is the time to decide if this is the type of person you would like to marry. The big questions about spiritual compatibility, life direction, and compatible lifestyles are addressed before courting begins. Courting is primarily about seeing if the two fit romantically and want to be married.

During the season of courting, there is a strong emphasis on accountability, transparency, and guarding your heart. Alone time is frowned upon, and mentoring with an older married couple is recommended. Because of the extended friendship phase—and all the time and preparation that went into the pre-courting phase—courting is usually much shorter than dating, lasting between six months and one year before engagement occurs.

While I have issues with the courting model, I recognize its positives, which I will discuss shortly. But overall, this model puts too much pressure on singles early in the connection. Many Christians who court avoid even interacting with the opposite sex, because they don't want to get attached to or lead on someone they won't marry. Courting beliefs and practices greatly limit interactions between singles.

Those who religiously follow the courting model are notoriously single for much longer, not only because they interact with the opposite sex less, but because their standards and expectations are often much higher than those who practice Christian dating. Christian courting may promote purity more than dating does, but it also hinders healthy relationship experiences. Courting promotes unrealistic expectations, because you think about the opposite sex far more than you interact with them. Social skills needed for a successful relationship are not developed until much later, and many enter a courting relationship with lots of false ideas.

Especially for adults, courting is pretty restrictive. I'm not saying it's a perfect model for younger Christians, but I do think it's more relevant for them. It's not surprising that Joshua Harris was only twenty-one when he wrote *I Kissed Dating Goodbye.* He also came out of a homeschool environment. I'm not dissing homeschool; we currently homeschool our kids. I'm saying this because a twenty-one-year-old unmarried guy, who was only a few years removed from being homeschooled, was bound to inject a lot of personal bias into his relationship advice, making it unhelpful to large swaths of the Christian singles community, especially those who are in a different season of life.

I'm not saying all twenty-one-year-olds are foolish and clueless about relationships. But it's unwise to give advice about a season of life you've not lived through yourself, especially when dealing with subjective topics like dating and courting. If advice is biblical, it doesn't matter who is giving the advice. Biblical truth is biblical truth. But courting and dating are not clear biblical topics, so personal bias will play a role in the advice given.

Even though I'm writing this book at the age of thirty-five, have been married for thirteen years, and have spent years working with singles in the area of dating, I freely admit my personal bias too. My opinions are influenced by my personal experiences, which are different from the experiences of many other Christians. So be careful about creating laws and rules for pursuing marriage out of points of application I'm making. Instead, seek the Spirit's leading as you apply biblical truth in the best way you can to your unique life (Gal. 5:25).

This makes me think of the strong warning from Jesus in Matthew 15:7–9: "You hypocrites! Well did Isaiah prophesy of you, when he said: 'This people honors me with their lips, but their heart is far from me; in vain do they worship me, teaching as doctrines the commandments of men.'" May we be careful not to create dating doctrines and teach them as God's commandments. May we follow the Lord with our hearts.

In reality, courting has more roots in conservative culture than it does in the Bible. If you are in your late teens or early twenties, and you have a strong Christian conservative community around you, perhaps courting will work well for you. It's not all bad, but it's definitely not the only biblical path toward marriage.

What Is Christian Dating?

Most of you are probably familiar with what the term *Christian dating* implies in Christian circles, so I won't say too much about it.

There are variations, depending on the church, but the rules of Christian dating are basically the same as secular dating, minus anything sinful, like premarital sex or living together.

Christian dating usually starts by a man and woman going on a few dates. At this point, the commitment level is low, and the two are getting to know each other better to see if they would like to become boyfriend and girlfriend. This phase has names like "just talking" or "going on dates," which is different from "dating." It's common for people to be going on dates or "talking to" multiple people at the same time. The relationship becomes exclusive when the man and woman become an official couple, only then calling each other boyfriend and girlfriend. Now they are dating.

Many people date for fun and do not think too far into the future. In other words, the dating mindset, unlike the courting mindset, often values the relationship between boyfriend and girlfriend in itself, rather than seeing it as merely a prelude to marriage. In the dating model, *marriage* is a scary word to hear too soon.

Dating can progress through phases (see chapter 11 for more on this). When the dating relationship begins, it's usually considered "not serious." After six months to a year, the relationship may be considered "getting more serious." And within a few years, the couple is considered "serious." The longer the dating relationship lasts, the more serious the relationship is considered. Eventually, the couple may decide to get engaged and then married. For most Christians, the dating process takes between two and four years.

One common problem that occurs in Christian dating is that people neglect to guard their hearts. By jumping into the romance phase more quickly, it is easier to get your hopes up and be hurt when things don't work out. Having more freedom to date whoever you want, without testing that person first in friendship, brings with it a higher risk of bad dating experiences. And since accountability and Christian community are not as emphasized in dating, the likelihood of sexual promiscuity is often greater than in courting.

Those who date, however, are usually more comfortable around the opposite sex and have healthier, more realistic views on relationships. The experiences they have in dating prepare them and give them relationship skills that will benefit them in marriage.

All that to say, dating is more liberal than courting, and these liberties bring both bad variables and good variables into relationships.

The Hybrid Approach

Everyone should pray and decide what they believe is the most biblical, wise, and relevant way to interact with someone on their journey toward marriage. What follows is advice I have found to be most useful for the majority of Christians. But since you are a unique individual, ask the Holy Spirit to guide you.

I'll use the term *dating* rather than *courting*, even though I take principles from both approaches, because dating is the term most people use, and courting has a specific definition.

In summary, I like the heart behind courting and the methods behind dating. I like that courting is marriage focused; I don't believe that having a boyfriend or girlfriend is a sufficient goal for a relationship. I consider dating to date unwise, because there is no biblical example of a long-term, healthy, romantic relationship other than marriage. Dating to date encourages intimacy without the safety of commitment found in marriage.

Intimacy without commitment leads to sin and getting hurt. As intimacy grows, commitment should grow at an equal rate. The greatest levels of intimacy should only be experienced in marriage, because marriage offers the greatest level of commitment.

So I like that courting is marriage focused, but I don't like the methods the courting model requires. Rather than courting only the one you expect to marry, I think it is wiser to date and get to know people who could be the one—depending on whether you are prepared to get married if God does reveal the one to you. In other words, before dating someone, you should be mature enough to get married if God does reveal they are the one. However, I don't believe you need to feel like this person is probably the one before dating them.

This is why, like the courting model suggests, I don't think most high school students should date. If you date before you are prepared to marry, you may be dating a long time, which can lead to higher intimacy than commitment. Sin and wounds then occur.

I think it's impossible to date someone long term (more than three or four years) and it remain a healthy relationship. Healthy relationships are always growing, and a dating relationship that continues too long always leads to an intimacy-commitment mismatch. A man and woman who love each other should grow more emotionally connected as time progresses. But there's a level of emotional intimacy that is unhealthy if it is not paired with the lifelong vows of marriage. And usually when these emotional bonds are growing strong, the physical pull toward sexual expression of these bonds gets too difficult to resist. Therefore, dating too long without getting married usually ends badly, because God did not design romantic love to thrive outside of the protection marriage alone provides.

This is how God made it! A man and woman who can date and resist having sex with each other for years probably have something missing in their relationship. God made a man and woman to connect so deeply and emotionally that they express this sexually. If things are healthy between the two of you, you will grow. But if you grow too intimate in dating, your relationship becomes unhealthy. The only solution is to date toward marriage or toward breaking up. Dating to date always leads to problems.

I like the freedom and the method of connecting that the traditional dating model offers. Two Christian adults who love Jesus should be mature enough to go on a date with the intention of seeing if there is romantic chemistry, without instantly falling into sin like premarital sex. If you know yourself, and you know you can't handle the freedom of going on a date with someone you don't know that well, that's fine. Do what works for you. But I believe many Christian singles take relationships too seriously too soon.

One of the biggest blockers to romance forming is the pressure for romance to form. The methods in dating put less pressure on single Christians, and thus I think it's wiser for them to use the dating methodology rather than the courting methodology. But the motive for marriage and the intentionality of the courting model to pursue marriage help singles avoid the mess of dating just to date.

So my advice is to take the best from both camps to form your own hybrid approach to dating.

Learn to Swim instead of Fearing the Water

Many of you have been hurt in relationships, and many others of you are hurt because you haven't had any relationship experience. Dating can be scary, because the dangers are real. You can hurt yourself if you date the wrong person. You can hurt someone you care about if you aren't mature enough. But being passive is dangerous too. You will feel lonely if you are doing things that are blocking you from the opposite sex. If you want to be married one day, you can't let these types of fears prevent you from pursuing it.

Rather than avoiding fear, it's far healthier to learn to thrive in the environment you fear. It's good to fear bodies of water if you can't swim, because you could drown. But the solution is not to avoid bodies of water your whole life. The solution is to learn to swim.

Yes, dating is very alluring, and it can be fun. But it's also a dangerous environment, and you can really get hurt. Don't throw caution to the wind. Don't rush in with no training. Don't live recklessly. Put boundaries around dating so you don't fall into something you can't handle. But also, don't live in fear. Don't be so afraid of love that you live a lonely life. Learn how to interact with the opposite sex. Learn how to date in a mature way that allows you to guard your heart while also connecting your heart with someone at an appropriate speed. Always keep intimacy and commitment congruent. Learn to swim.

As intimacy grows, commitment should grow at an equal rate. The greatest levels of intimacy should only be experienced in marriage, because marriage offers the greatest level of commitment.

We'll continue this learning process in the chapters ahead. But don't worry about "doing it right." If you disagree with some of my opinions, that's okay! What's most important is that you are walking with God and learning how to love others in a biblical way. Do everything in faith:

> Therefore let us not pass judgment on one another any longer, but rather decide never to put a stumbling block or hindrance in the way of a brother.…
>
> The faith that you have, keep between yourself and God. Blessed is the one who has no reason to pass judgment on himself for what he approves. But whoever has doubts is condemned if he eats, because the eating is not from faith. For whatever does not proceed from faith is sin. (Rom. 14:13, 22–23)

Likewise, do what the Holy Spirit is convicting you to do. Whatever approach you choose, do it in faith. Dating will look different from couple to couple; just make sure your main aim is to glorify God.

10

RISK IS REQUIRED

When Bethany and I were dating, we enjoyed rock climbing together. Bethany's dad had been taking her since she was a kid, and I had learned the basics working at a summer camp. I wanted to learn more, so Bethany set up a climbing trip in Kentucky with her dad, where he could give me more advanced training.

That trip was humbling! My rock-climbing experience had been limited to indoor gyms, and I quickly learned that climbing on real rock was a lot harder. Bethany scrambled up the same routes that I struggled on. She was way better than me. My only saving grace was that I had brought a friend who was even worse than me. Thanks, wingman!

Despite my humiliation, I stuck with it. That trip to Kentucky was only the first of many. When Bethany and I were newly married, we spent a lot of weekends meeting up with her dad to climb. We all bonded together, and over the years, I learned a lot about climbing from my father-in-law. Now I have enough knowledge for Bethany and me to go safely climbing ourselves.

You can draw a lot of parallels between learning to rock climb and learning to date. Like dating, rock climbing can be as adventurous as you want. There are many forms of rock climbing, like there are many ways to pursue marriage. In rock climbing, there is always a trade-off between adventure and safety. The safer you make it with ropes and anchors, the less it feels like rock climbing. Each climber decides their own comfort level.

Likewise, if you date in a guarded way, you may feel safer, but you also remove some of the excitement, which can stall a relationship permanently. If you take unwise risks in relationships, you may experience some additional excitement, but you are much more likely to be injured. Each person needs to find that healthy dating space where they embrace the risks while not recklessly hurting themselves and others. This will look different from person to person, because we all have different comfort levels and convictions.

For me, embracing some meaningful risk is the best way to date, because if you play it too safe, you won't allow space for love to grow. At the same time, you don't want to "free solo."

If you date in a guarded way, you may feel safer, but you also remove some of the excitement, which can stall a relationship permanently.

The Academy Award–winning documentary *Free Solo* followed climber Alex Honnold on his free-solo climb (meaning without any safety equipment whatsoever) of the 3,000-foot El Capitan route in Yosemite National Park.

While I enjoyed the documentary, it gives people an unrealistic idea of rock climbing. In reality, Alex Honnold is a complete outlier in the world of climbing. Other climbers can climb the same routes, but they use ropes. Other climbers do free solo, but only on less difficult routes.

While Alex is incredible to watch, he is an unfair example of a rock climber. He is quite literally the only person in the world who can climb the way he does. If you try to learn climbing by watching him, you'll either give up before your first climb or you'll die on your first try. You and I can't climb like Alex. No one else can.

There is a similar peril in forming relationship expectations based on what you see on TV or the movie screen. Like seeing Alex Honnold rock climbing, we cannot expect to learn much that is relevant to our lives and relationships by watching actors on a screen. When we develop relationship expectations from TV, movies, or romance novels, we see all the fun and excitement; we rarely see the dangers and consequences of the unwise risks.

When I learned to climb, I was mentored by someone who had been doing it for years. My father-in-law showed me the realistic steps to take. He taught me how to assess a route to know if I could do it or not. He demonstrated how to use ropes and anchors for safety. In short, he showed me the process all climbers go through to learn the sport.

Alex Honnold went through these steps too; he just progressed further than anyone else. He didn't roll out of bed one day and decide he would free solo one of the hardest rock climbs in the world. But this is the approach many people take to romance.

If you try to find love like the movies portray it, you'll either give up because you know you can't live up to that ideal or you'll take unwise risks and die an emotional death in the process. Movies mostly show people thriving in relationships while rejecting God's rules to keep people safe. They never show the aftermath of ignoring God's loving guidance in relationships. There is a process of spiritual growth that is required to embrace the needed risks in relationships, while also taking the necessary safety precautions to remain alive.

Men and women need time in each season together so they can properly prepare for the next season. The seasons build on each other. The speed of each season can vary from relationship to relationship, but you can identify general themes across the board. If you don't respect the necessary phases to dating, if you don't learn from others, if you rush the process and take too many unwise risks, you'll never safely arrive at the top of any relationship mountain. If you want to enjoy romance and remain safe in the process, you must respect the phases of a healthy dating relationship.

God has not given us a rigid blueprint for how every Christian couple should pursue marriage. However, through applying biblical wisdom and observing real life, it becomes clear there are common seasons a couple must go through as they discern the will of God for their relationship. Like someone trying to skip the learning process in rock climbing, it becomes extremely dangerous when people try to bypass necessary relationship seasons.

"Respect the edge" is a climbing safety motto that has stuck with me. It means when you are near the edge of a cliff, don't disrespect it by being careless regarding safety. It's not a game. One slip without a rope, and you die. But the motto isn't "Avoid the edge." Rock climbing takes place on the edge. It is meant to be adventurous but not a death wish. It's important to "respect the edge" in dating too. Relationships always involve risk, but you don't need to risk everything.

Love without risk is not love. To love is to risk getting hurt, because when you open your heart, you become receptive to both joy and pain. If you open yourself to anything authentic, you will get the whole spectrum of reality. The sun shines, but the rains come too. But if you stay inside forever, what's the point in living? The only way to avoid relationship pain is to avoid love. But that is a meaningless life (1 Cor. 13:1–3).

So we don't want to avoid romance, but we do need to respect romance. Relationships are not a game. Your heart is on the line, and so is someone else's. It's easy to get overconfident with the heights you are soaring to and then slip to an emotional death because you became careless about guarding your heart (Prov. 4:23).

Ropes, anchors, a climbing harness—no matter what type of climb you are doing, there are core elements that must be present if you prefer not to die. If you are overly obsessed with safety, however, you'll diminish the joy of climbing. Likewise, no matter what path you take in your pursuit of marriage, there are some core relationship qualities that must be present if you want to have a biblical relationship while guarding your heart. But if you try too hard to be safe, you may ruin the joy of the relationship.

In this chapter, I want to give couples advice on embracing the necessary risks involved in dating while respecting God's rules for pursuing marriage that will keep you safe. Like my father-in-law mentored me in rock climbing, my goal is to help you learn to guard your heart so you can enjoy pursuing marriage while minimizing risk.

Guard Your Heart without Walling It Off

"Above all else, guard your heart, for everything you do flows from it" (Prov. 4:23 NIV). Many people wrongly interpret this famous proverb to mean "Wall off your heart and protect yourself at all costs."

If you don't guard your heart, you may get hurt by people who have bad intentions for you. But if you wall your heart off completely, you will never have the chance to be loved by someone with good intentions. While we need healthy boundaries to guard our hearts in dating, a boundary need not be an impenetrable wall.

Imagine your house to be your heart, and your bedroom the deepest place in your heart. The property outside your house is your whole life. Your first line of defense at home may be a fence around your property line. But somewhere in that fence is a gate. From the gate, perhaps there is a path that leads to your front door. The front door has a lock that can help regulate who enters your house. Inside, you have a bedroom, your most personal space. Not everyone who makes it into your house needs to be in your bedroom.

In the pre-dating phase, you may welcome people you like onto your property (let them into your life) but not into your house (your heart) yet. Once you start dating someone, you invite them into your house (your heart), just not your bedroom (the deepest place in your heart). If you two get married, then you invite them into your bedroom (the deepest place in your heart).

To guard your heart, you need levels of guardedness appropriate to the levels of your relationship. Your first boundary should not be at your bedroom door. Don't let a stranger into your heart, much less the deepest place in your heart. But also, don't keep someone you are supposedly dating outside of your fence, looking at your heart from the public sidewalk. As your mutual trust and commitment levels increase, your emotional intimacy should increase as well, culminating with the highest level of commitment (marriage) opening the door to the deepest place in your heart.

One of the ways Christians often try to protect their hearts is by creating lists of requirements. But these lists can often create unhealthy boundaries. A list with unrealistic requirements will keep people away who should be allowed closer to you. A list with too few requirements will allow people close to you who should be kept away from you.

A person's list of requirements is often a list of ways they've been hurt. When someone hurts us, we create new requirements to try to avoid getting hurt again. With each hurtful relationship experience, our list gets longer until, instead of looking for a real person, we are looking for a person who doesn't exist. We create a list only a perfect person could fulfill.

While Christians should marry someone who wants to live like Jesus, there is only one Jesus! We need him to be our Perfect One so we can be secure enough to give imperfect love to an imperfect person. In this life, we won't be perfect, and neither will anyone else (Rom. 3:23, 1 John 1:8). Only Jesus can solve the issues in our hearts. Christian marriage is a partnership between two people who can worship Jesus together for all that he's done for them.

Thus, our list of requirements often becomes a set of barriers to a relationship. If you look for a perfect person to complete you, you will be endlessly searching and always incomplete. If you accept that real people have both good qualities and bad qualities, you can meet someone who will be an immense source of joy, as God intends a spouse to be. Safety and risk are both required for healthy romance. Too much safety and you will smother the flame. Too much risk and you may get burned.

A list with unrealistic requirements will keep people away who should be allowed closer to you. A list with too few requirements will allow people close to you who should be kept away from you.

While I think it's certainly healthy to have *some* personal preferences a real person can live up to, be careful you are not importing unrealistic expectations from watching romantic comedies and trying to re-create those imaginary love stories in your own life. Preferences are fine. But limit your absolutes to a very few requirements.

Four Biblical Absolutes for a Successful Marriage

While you may think of additional requirements, here are four things God wants all Christians to possess and to look for in another person when dating for the purpose of considering marriage.

1. Being a Christian

This is the clearest biblical requirement for Christian marriage, but oddly, many Christians struggle the most with this one.

First Corinthians 15:33 says, "Do not be deceived: 'Bad company ruins good morals.'" Paul specifically said not to deceive ourselves about our ability to be good people when we're constantly with bad company. We may act like we are the special ones who can easily resist temptation. It's just not true. Stay long enough around people who are pulling us down, and we are bound to fall.

Try standing on a chair and pulling someone up on it with you. Then stand on a chair and ask that same person to try pulling you off. Which one took less effort? It's far easier for the non-Christian to pull the Christian down in dating than it is for the Christian to pull the non-Christian up. God's rule about Christians marrying Christians is not meant to steal your joy but to protect you and increase your joy.

First Corinthians 7:39 says, "A wife is bound to her husband as long as he lives. But if her husband dies, she is free to be married to whom she wishes, only in the Lord." There it is in black-and-white lettering—"free to be married to whom she wishes, only in the Lord."

Some people challenge this requirement of Christians only marrying others "in the Lord." One reason they give is because Paul instructed women who were already married to unbelievers to remain married, unless the husbands showed they did not want to continue living with their wives (1 Cor. 7:13–16).

In some situations people become Christians after they are already married, and many times only one of the spouses chooses to believe in Jesus. This was especially common in Paul's day, because the gospel was just beginning to spread. Paul's advice to a Christian who is already married to an unbeliever is not justification to marry an unbeliever. Since Paul clearly said that Christians should only marry "in the Lord" (1 Cor. 7:39), we know that his words elsewhere would not state the opposite. The Bible never contradicts itself.

Additionally, it's worth noting that when Paul talked about a believer being married to an unbeliever, he gave them counsel about their desire to get divorced. This implies that it was common for these unequally yoked spouses to be unhappy together. Why else would Paul need to address divorce with unequally yoked spouses?

Paul said when your marriage is hard because you're married to an unbeliever, this doesn't give you the right to bail. If you want to avoid this situation, obey God's loving instructions about being equally yoked:

> Do not be unequally yoked with unbelievers. For what partnership has righteousness with lawlessness? Or what fellowship has light with darkness? What accord has Christ with Belial? Or what portion does a believer share with an unbeliever? (2 Cor. 6:14–15)

An ox needs to be yoked with an ox of similar size and strength, or else they struggle to plow together—one dragging the other, creating unnecessary stress. But when you put two similar oxen together, they plow much better with less stress. Likewise, God has work for you to do (Eph. 2:10). You want to marry someone who can work with rather than against you.

Second Corinthians 6:14–15 does not specifically mention marriage, but I can't think of a stronger yoke than the covenant bond of marriage. Therefore, I don't see how you could read these verses and then think a Christian is free to marry a non-Christian.

So, Christians are not biblically free to marry unbelievers. But what about dating? While dating is not as strong a yoke as marriage, it still yokes you to some degree. Therefore, in my opinion, dating an unbeliever is being unequally yoked.

Since the Bible doesn't specifically say that dating is a yoke, some will argue it's okay to date unbelievers. After all, you could be a witness as you date them. We all have that one Christian friend who dated an unbeliever, the unbeliever became a Christian, and then they got married. If it worked for a friend, why wouldn't it work for me? From my experience, people cling to a question like this when trying to justify something the Holy Spirit is telling them not to do.

Missionary dating, dating an unbeliever while trying to convert them, is an unwise practice. While some people have come to faith through dating a believer, there are far more Christians who have been dragged away from God through dating unbelievers. For every one story of missionary dating working, I hear a hundred stories of it blowing up in people's faces.

Not that Christians should be isolationists (Matt. 28:19–20). We are called to be a light to the world (Matt. 5:14–16). But we are also warned not to be friends with the world: "You adulterous people! Do you not know that friendship with the world is enmity with God? Therefore whoever wishes to be a friend of the world makes himself an enemy of God" (James 4:4). Jesus came into the world to save sinners (1 Tim. 1:15), but he was cautious who he opened himself up to: "But Jesus on his part did not entrust himself to them, because he knew all people and needed no one to bear witness about man, for he himself knew what was in man" (John 2:24–25).

Jesus witnessed to, served, and spent time with unbelievers. But serving and giving are different than receiving from unbelievers. When you are friends with or dating someone, you are not only ministering to them; you are also receiving from them. You can serve anyone. You can witness to anyone. But as Christians, we are not called to be open to everyone, receiving what they are giving. We can be friendly to non-Christians, but we are not called to be true, deep friends with people who don't love Jesus. Jesus did not open himself to the world, but he did to his twelve: "No longer do I call you servants, for the servant does not know what his master is doing; but I have called you friends, for all that I have heard from my Father I have made known to you" (John 15:15). And even among the twelve he had his inner circle of Peter, James, and John.

Missionary dating is a bad idea because it unequally yokes you (2 Cor. 6:14–15), makes you close friends with an unbeliever (James 4:4; 1 John 2:15), and causes you to be around temptation rather than fleeing it (1 Cor. 6:18; 2 Tim. 2:22). With these biblical truths in mind, how can you call the unbeliever you're dating to obey God's word when your relationship is in defiance of God's word? When you missionary date, you teach an unbeliever you can follow God in your own way rather than in obedience to God's word.

But what about all those couples that it worked for? In Numbers 20, God told Moses to speak to a rock so water would come out of it for the people. Instead, Moses struck the rock twice. God was displeased with Moses' disobedience and then prevented him from entering the Promised Land. But he still allowed the water to come out of the rock for the people. Successfully accomplishing what you want to accomplish is not always a sign that you are in God's will. Moses reaped the consequences of his disobedience. It would have been much better if he had done it God's way.

Likewise, God doesn't need our disobedience to save someone. God can save an unbeliever without you dating them. And God can put you together when you are equally yoked. If you disrespect this order, you will get hurt. There are always good reasons for God's commands.

For example, brand-new Christians are unlikely to have the maturity to resist sexual temptation in the dating season. Sexual sin during the dating phase will affect the marriage season. The more mature Christian in such a relationship may have to endure growing pains because of their partner's lack of Christian maturity, especially if the new believer did not have a season of growth in their relationship with God before entering into a dating relationship. God's grace will redeem all our sins, but we inflict trials on ourselves when we deviate from God's ways.

When we disobey God's word, there is always a natural consequence. While God forgives us and turns our evil mistakes into good through the gospel of Jesus Christ, there are still natural consequences. For example, with the sin of gluttony, God will instantly forgive you if you confess, but the abuse your body has gone through because of overeating won't suddenly vanish. I can't overeat for years, confess this sin, and then get mad at God when I don't wake up with six-pack abs the next day. Sadly, this is what many people do with relationships. They ignore God's rules, confess their sins, and then blame God when things are not instantly better: "When a man's folly brings his way to ruin, his heart rages against the LORD" (Prov. 19:3).

Therefore, if someone missionary dates and it "works out," while God was pleased to use his grace to create a good result, negative consequences will come to bear for the sinful actions.

Additionally, while it is impossible to know if someone will turn from the faith and prove they were never saved (1 John 2:19), there is a higher probability of a new professing Christian to turn from the faith in comparison with someone who has a track record of faithfulness. Perseverance and endurance are the marks of true believers, and these can only be revealed over time. While there is no guarantee that the person you marry will remain faithful to Jesus, there is a greater likelihood of a mature professing Christian remaining faithful to God. Therefore, marrying a new professing believer puts you at greater risk of being married to someone who will turn out to be no Christian at all.

Lastly, missionary dating is a bad idea because a healthy relationship cannot be built around changing someone. Would you want someone to date you and then say, "Hey, I like your potential, but I'm also going to need you to change your core beliefs if you want to stay with me. Can you do that for me but also convince me you are doing this for yourself so it doesn't feel like you are just faking it for me?" Never make someone's potential the deciding factor in your decision-making process. When someone has potential, it also means they may never reach their potential. Relationship decisions should be made with present reality, not potential, in mind.

A healthy relationship focuses on learning what the person has gone through, enjoying them for who God made them to be, and encouraging them to keep growing in the ways the Holy Spirit is leading them to grow. Missionary dating creates an environment where you are the counselor and your boyfriend or girlfriend is the counselee. This produces an unhealthy dynamic in the relationship and prevents mutual support and respect.

In short, missionary dating creates a mess that can be avoided. Do it God's way. He can save someone without you disobeying his commands. Don't sacrifice your relationship with Jesus to gain a relationship with someone else.

2. Producing the Fruits of the Spirit

According to Scripture, true Christians are not necessarily all those who have prayed the sinner's prayer. We are not saved by works but by grace alone. And saving grace always comes with faith, and faith without works is dead (1 Cor. 15:10; James 2:17). Ephesians 2:8–10 says:

> For by grace you have been saved through faith. And this is not your own doing; it is the gift of God, not a result of works, so that no one may boast. For we are his workmanship, created in Christ Jesus for good works, which God prepared beforehand, that we should walk in them.

We are saved "by grace," "through faith," and "for good works." Churches have proclaimed Ephesians 2:8–9 loudly, but sadly verse 10 is often forgotten. If your salvation is not accompanied with works, the Bible says you should question your salvation (2 Cor.

13:5; James 2:17). We are not called to judge each other's hearts, but we are called to assess people's behavior to see whether their actions back up their words (1 Cor. 5:11–13; Gal. 5:19–24).

It's not enough only to date people who claim to be Christian. Anyone can claim that label. We have to use the definition outlined in the Bible—a Christian is someone who follows Christ. Praying before meals, listening to Christian music, and even going to church every week are good things, but they are not enough evidence someone is a Christian. A Christian will exhibit the fruit of the Spirit in their life (Gal. 5:22–24).

3. Prepared to Fulfill the Biblical Role of a Husband or Wife

Many Christians genuinely exhibit the fruit of the Spirit but are still not ready to date.

As I mentioned in chapter 9, I believe in a hybrid approach to dating, where we take traditional courting principles and pair them with traditional dating methods. You don't need to know if you want to marry the person you are dating, because that is the question you are trying to answer in dating. But you should be in a season of life where you are prepared to get married if God shows you this person is the one. Likewise, you should only date people who are also prepared to get married.

Therefore, as you connect with someone in dating, you should look for evidence that they are prepared to fulfill the biblical role of a husband or wife. I'm not going to explore those roles in detail here, because that is a big topic that goes beyond the scope of this book.

Whether you are complementarian and you believe the husband and wife have equally important but different, defined roles, or an egalitarian and you believe the husband and wife can freely divide up marriage roles as best fits their gifts and personalities, every Christian agrees that husbands and wives take on a role in marriage that they did not have when they were single.

Study the Bible on this topic. Read Ephesians 5:21–33, 1 Peter 3:1–7, and the many other passages about marriage. Decide what you believe the Bible says about the marriage roles for a husband and wife. And then make sure the person you are dating is able and enthusiastic to fulfill their role, if you did decide to marry them. If you know they are not prepared for this, stop dating them. Don't date someone based on potential but on who they are right now.

If you are dating an unbeliever or an immature Christian, hoping that one day they will transform into the mature spouse you desire them to be, you are hoping to marry someone who does not currently exist. This is called fantasizing. Look for the person who actually is what you hope them to be, because that person actually exists.

Don't date someone based on potential but on who they are right now.

Of course, we should all be growing and maturing (2 Pet. 1:8). If you decide to marry someone, ideally you both will be different people in ten years because you've grown so much. But don't let your baseline requirements for marriage dip below what the Bible requires. If you don't see evidence for Christlikeness in dating, don't expect it to magically appear in marriage.

4. Having Mutual Love and a Willingness to Commit in Marriage

Marriage is not a biblical command for all Christians. It is a biblical option for those Christians who have this calling. One sign that you are called to marriage is having the desire to be married.

Paul was called to be single, and thus he was happy to be single, which is why he said, "I wish that all were as I myself am" (1 Cor. 7:7a). But he also knew others would have a different call, which is why he added, "But each has his own gift from God, one of one kind and one of another" (1 Cor. 7:7b). Throughout 1 Corinthians 7, he laid out the principle that a desire to be married should be pursued rather than denied:

- But because of the temptation to sexual immorality, each man should have his own wife and each woman her own husband. (verse 2)
- But if they cannot exercise self-control, they should marry. For it is better to marry than to burn with passion. (verse 9)
- If anyone thinks that he is not behaving properly toward his betrothed, if his passions are strong, and it has to be, let him do as he wishes: let them marry—it is no sin. (verse 36)

When choosing marriage or singleness in general, personal choice is a big variable to consider. Likewise, when we apply these general principles about choosing singleness or marriage to the specific choice of remaining single or marrying a particular person, personal choice is a big variable to consider here too!

Someone can have the first three of the biblical traits that would make a great spouse (being a Christian, bearing fruit for Jesus, and being prepared to fulfill the marriage role) and still not be the one God has for you. This is why a healthy period of dating is important. Sometimes two great individuals are not great together. When God confirms that he wants you to marry the person you are dating, you both will want to marry each other.

The Bible doesn't put an unrealistic set of demands on Christians when it comes to marriage: Christians can only marry Christians, real Christians bear fruit for God, marriage requires a husband and wife to fulfill certain marriage roles, and the man and woman should want to marry each other.

These four simple rules will keep you safe, but they won't take away all the risk required to have a genuine relationship with someone.

11

THE EIGHT PHASES OF A HEALTHY RELATIONSHIP

When Bethany and I were going through premarital counseling, our mentor couple gave us some resources by Dave Ramsey.

As we worked through the content together, this couple showed us how they managed their finances, so we had a good model to follow. They answered our questions about investing, and they encouraged us to make wise financial decisions. By God's grace, we've been able to follow Dave Ramsey's famous "7 Baby Steps," and this has been a huge blessing to us over the years.

Money and relationships share a lot of similarities. You can spend a lot of time learning about the multifaceted topic of money. When you talk to someone who really loves investing in the stock market, for example, it can make your head spin. But money doesn't need to be complicated. There are common principles that normal people like you and me can understand and do: avoid debt, save for what you want, work hard, plan ahead, and so on. Along the same line, relationships can be super intricate if you want to dive into the psychology. But they need not be complicated if you follow some basic biblical truths: avoid relationship debt, work hard, plan ahead, and so on.

In this chapter, we'll discuss the phases wise Christians embrace during a dating relationship. Just like getting out of debt and building wealth, following some basic principles and steps in relationships can really help. As Dave Ramsey helped me with his 7 Baby Steps, I want to help you understand a simple path for building relationship wealth.

Have people become wealthy who did not follow Ramsey's 7 Baby Steps? Of course! But over the decades, Ramsey noticed common themes among people who were good with money, and he identified some biblical principles that revolutionized people's finances.

Likewise, you can marry someone and have a healthy relationship even if you don't follow the steps I'm going to talk about in this chapter. However, I've witnessed many couples using these steps in dating, and they are reaping the benefits in marriage. There are also some key biblical principles you need to follow as you date someone if you want to avoid unhealthy relationship debt.

Before I break down these Eight Dating Steps, let me first encourage you to be a relationship investor rather than a relationship debtor.

Emotional Investing versus Emotional Debt

In finance, people often confuse good investing and bad debt. Good investing is when you use your resources to gain even more resources.

Bad debt is when you borrow what you don't have to gain what you can't afford. Investing brings you more. Debt leaves you with less.

Buying a house, for example, almost always requires a loan. If you have an investment mindset, you only borrow money you can afford to pay back monthly, while leaving enough for the rest of your needs. You also are careful to get a good interest rate on your loan. Ideally, the value of your house will appreciate over time. In addition, as you pay off your mortgage, you will have equity in the house and property. Buying a house can be a good investment if done properly.

If, however, you buy a house that requires a higher monthly payment than you can afford, and if you unwisely sign a contract with a terrible interest rate, and if the house doesn't appreciate over time, it could turn into bad debt, leaving you with less than you put in.

While investing and debt both require you to sacrifice something to gain something, investing requires thoughtful planning, while debt comes from thoughtless spending. Both require an up-front cost, but the results are very different.

Investing always carries the risk that it won't work, but if it fails, you are not sunk, because you were investing capital, not going into debt. You may need to take time to rebuild capital before you invest again, but it's manageable and repeatable, unlike debilitating debt. Investors assess their investment and back out if they realize it is not going to pay off. Debtors can't get out, because they got in too deep and are now trapped: "The borrower is the slave of the lender" (Prov. 22:7). Eventually, an investor finds an investment that pays off. Their resources multiply and bring them a return, rather than endlessly taking, like debt does.

Christian dating is best approached with an investor's mindset, not a debtor's mindset. You need to have some personal equity built up before investing some in a relationship. If you are not whole, and you don't have a healthy heart, you don't yet have enough emotional resources to spare on a relationship investment. You need to take care of your basic emotional needs before getting involved with someone else.

Once you are healthy and walking with the Lord, you can then save enough emotional resources to risk investing when a good relationship opportunity comes along. But once you start investing, watch your investment closely, constantly gauging if you should get out and count your losses or invest more because it's going well. If it's turning out poorly, a good investor backs out before investing too much and going into debt. A good dater does the same. If the investment is going well, it deserves more capital, and more investment should be given. Similarly, if you are dating someone and the effort you are putting in is multiplying and growing into something really strong and solid, you should keep dating.

Debtors want what they can't have and spend what they don't possess to get it. Investors use what they have to gain more. Try to think like this in relationships. Is your dating relationship giving more than it is taking (investment), or is it taking more than it is giving (debt)? Each person in the relationship should be giving equally to the other, and the efforts of each producing good in the other's life.

While Jesus used finances as the foundation for his parable in Matthew 25:14–30, his main point went far beyond money. In verses 15–18, he said:

> To one he gave five talents, to another two, to another one, to each according to his ability. Then he went away. He who had received the five talents went at once and traded with them, and he made five talents more. So also he who had the two talents made two talents more. But he who had received the one talent went and dug in the ground and hid his master's money.

When the master returned, he commended the servants who had invested their money and made him even more. But when the master confronted the third servant, he launched into a different response:

> You wicked and slothful servant! You knew that I reap where I have not sown and gather where I scattered no seed? Then you ought to have invested my money with the bankers, and at my coming I should have received what was my own with interest. (verses 26–27)

What's wild is that this servant didn't even lose his master's money! In Matthew 25:25, the servant said to his master, "Here, you have what is yours." We can infer, therefore, that the master might have been less angry with this servant had he at least tried to invest it and failed rather than not trying at all. The master knew this servant didn't have great ability, because he had given out the money "each according to his ability." But when the master scolded the servant, he didn't blame him for a lack of ability but for being "wicked and slothful" (Matt. 25:26).

We all need to take Jesus' warning seriously. Many seem to think the goal of life is to not mess up what God has given us. We try to guard our hearts, avoid getting hurt, and return to God what he has given us. But that isn't all God wants. Like the lazy servant who avoided using what God had given him, if we bury our hearts in the ground and don't use our lives to bring glory to God through loving him and others, we are like this third servant.

God has given you life and love, and he wants you to invest that life and love so you are producing more for his glory. He wants you to take what you have been given and use it to produce even more for him. He wants you to invest.

The first servant took the five talents and "traded with them" (Matt. 25:16) to gain his master more. The second servant "who had the two talents made two talents more" (verse 17). It doesn't specifically say how he did that, just that he did. When the master spoke to the third servant, he didn't say he should have traded his one talent, like the first servant. He said, if nothing else, the servant should have given it to the bankers to earn interest (verse 27).

Each person in the relationship should be giving equally to the other, and the efforts of each producing good in the other's life.

The master was not overly concerned with the method his servants used to invest his money or even how much they earned. He just wanted them to be "good and faithful" (Matt. 25:21, 23) instead of "wicked and slothful" (verse 26). There are a lot of investment strategies, each with pros and cons; the main thing to look at is the bottom line.

Likewise, whatever steps you follow in your dating path, make sure you are not wasting the life and love God has given you to invest for his glory. Avoid going into debt for someone who is going to leave you worse than they found you. You may invest in some relationships that don't result in marriage, but you can avoid going into debilitating emotional debt if you follow wise steps through your dating relationships.

The Eight Dating Steps

In chapter 9, we said that a couple's intimacy should be congruent with their commitment level. This helps protect your hearts while also allowing your hearts to connect and grow as a couple. You need to bond, but you want to avoid bonding in ways that exceed the healthy limits of a dating relationship. When you give each other the full commitment only marriage can provide, then you can fully open your heart to the other person in the most intimate of ways.

We also talked about the need to assess. If you only connect with and never assess the other person and the relationship, you may miss red flags because you are wearing infatuation goggles. Infatuation goggles warp your vision and make you see what you want to see, rather than what is true. However, if you only assess, you will kill the relationship by starving it of the emotional connection it needs to grow.

Now let's bring in the Eight Dating Steps. To go from dating to engagement (steps 3–7), I recommend somewhere between six and twenty-four months. Go faster than six months, and you risk overlooking red flags. Go longer than two years, and you risk pretending you are married when you are not. These timeline suggestions are only my opinion and for relatively normal circumstances. But generally, I have found them to be healthy for most couples.

In the pages ahead I will unpack each step, but here's the full list so you can see them all at once:

Step 1. Pre-dating
Step 2. Defining the Relationship
Step 3. Dating (The first six months of the relationship)
Step 4. Moderately Serious Dating (Between months six and twelve of the relationship)
Step 5. Serious Dating (Between months six and twenty-four of the relationship)
Step 6. Pre-engagement (Between months six and twenty-four of the relationship)
Step 7. Engagement (Sometime after month six and before month twenty-four)
Step 8. Wedding Vows (No more than six months after getting engaged)

To help even out your intimacy and commitment levels, and to keep your assessment and connection balanced, I strongly encourage you to embrace these Eight Dating Steps.

Step 1. Pre-dating

Purpose: The goal of the pre-dating step is to learn if the other person is a professing Christian, is bearing fruit for God, and appears ready to fulfill the biblical role of a husband or wife. You also want to see some evidence that you like this person romantically and that they like you too.

Length: This phase can be as long or short as needed. If you are using online dating, you may accomplish this goal through a few online interactions and an initial date. At other times, this step can take years, especially if the two of you are friends and your feelings change over time.

Commitment: On a scale of 1 to 10, your commitment is at 0 in this step.

Additional Comments: Before you enter this phase, you should have done the internal heart preparation to be in a relationship. You want to be relatively mature in the Lord before getting involved with a potential dating partner. The information in section 1 of this book focuses on how to do this.

During this step, you get to know the other person. In the beginning, you may lack clarity about whether you should or would date the person if the opportunity arose. Traditionally, this step is accomplished through friendship. With online dating, this phase usually involves messaging with the person.

Before completing this step, you want to be reasonably sure the other person meets the minimum biblical requirements for the type of person God wants Christians to marry (see chapter 10). If they aren't a Christian, don't move ahead. If their life doesn't show clear evidence of being a faithful Christian, don't take the next step with them. And if they are displaying massive red flags about their readiness to fulfill the biblical role of a husband or wife, don't go any further with them.

You are not looking for 100 percent certainty of the person's biblical readiness for marriage at this point. You just want to weed out those who are obviously not biblically ready.

Finally, before moving ahead, you should be able to affirmatively answer the simple question "Do I want to date this person?" Do you enjoy their company? Do you like talking with them? Does it seem like there is romantic potential? Do you see the two of you as more than friends? For the dating journey to begin, you need evidence of a romantic connection that is getting harder to deny.

This season is best met with low expectations, high openness to interacting in lighthearted ways, and high guardedness toward connecting in deeply emotional and vulnerable ways.

Step 2. Defining the Relationship

Purpose: The goal of the defining the relationship step is to clearly transition from acquaintances or friends into something more through having a DTR (define the relationship) talk. The result of this talk might be going on dates or becoming boyfriend and girlfriend. The main thing is to have a clear conversation that defines where you two are at romantically.

Length: A DTR talk happens every time you need to transition into a new phase of a relationship.

Commitment: On a scale of 1 to 10, this is a 1.

Additional Comments: Step 2 is about verbalizing and clarifying romantic interest. A DTR talk can be lengthy or brief, so long as it clarifies the relationship status.

For example, if you are just friends, and you want to see if you connect romantically, you might say something like "Hey, I'm glad we're friends, but I've been wondering if there could be something more between us. Would you like to go on a date with me to explore the possibility?" That's it. Simple. Even though the statement is short and sweet, you've spoken the crucial word—*date*! A date is more than two friends hanging out. If, after a few dates, you connect well and want to be a couple, you'll need to have a second DTR talk to make sure you're both on the same page.

Or if you are good friends with someone, and you want to jump over the "going on dates" phase and enter into an exclusive couple relationship, you'll want to have a DTR talk then.

If you connect with someone online and then feel like you two should meet for a date, you need to have a quick DTR talk: "Hey, want to go on a date with me?" This clarifies that you are ready to take a small step forward. After going on enough dates to know you want to become boyfriend and girlfriend, you'll need to have another DTR talk to make this transition.

If you are a Christian woman who doesn't want to pursue a man, the DTR talk can be a tricky step. Ideally, the man initiates the DTR talks because they are essential to his pursuit. However, if the guy pursuing you is skipping the DTR talks, you may need to simply request one: "Hey, I'm really enjoying our time together, and I'd like to know how you see our relationship at this point. Can we talk about that?"

In a perfect world, a perfect man would clarify the relationship at the exact right time for the woman. But nothing, and no one, is perfect in this world. If you are a woman who runs into this problem, his unwise choice to skip DTR talks doesn't need to be a deal breaker, as long as he is continuing to actively pursue in other ways. Eventually, however, these talks need to happen. If he doesn't clarify things at a time that suits you, it's best to just go ahead and ask him. This gives him the opportunity to say how he feels before you do. The point is, if there's an elephant in the room, don't simply ignore it.

If you are a Christian man, be aware that most women appreciate the clarity a DTR talk brings. Even if she sees the relationship differently than you do, she will still respect you for being clear and not playing games. If you prefer to show her with your actions that you are interested, that is great. Don't be all talk. But most women value verbal affirmation that you are interested. They need the assurance that they are correctly interpreting your actions. The only way she can be sure of your intentions is if you communicate them verbally.

For more on this, refer back to the principles outlined in chapters 6 and 7.

Step 3. Dating

Purpose: Your main goal in the dating step is to clarify if God wants you to marry each other one day. When a dating relationship begins, your focus is to find further evidence to clarify the things you feel are true between the two of you or to find evidence that disproves what you hoped was true.

Length: A couple should try to extend this lighthearted, lower-commitment phase for at least six months before becoming moderately serious about marriage (step 4), but not much longer than a year. From the start of dating to engagement (steps 3–7), somewhere between six months and two years is usually best.

Commitment: On a scale of 1 to 10, this step is a 2 or 3.

Additional Comments: The dating step signals that you've moved past awkward unknowns and unclarified feelings to acknowledge that you like each other enough to move to a new level of commitment. By becoming an exclusive couple, you set aside time together to explore the possibility of becoming a husband and wife one day.

At this point in the relationship, it's best to avoid talking about marriage too much. While you both should be marriage focused and not "dating to date," you must respect the fact that you are a new couple. Like a tree just sprouting, you can't ask too much of the relationship just yet. Rather, focus on feeding and nourishing it to see whether it will grow and produce good fruit. Enjoy this new relationship, but don't smother it by getting too far ahead of reality.

During this season, it's best to avoid heavy conversations about important topics. It's not time yet to talk about whether you want kids, how many kids you want, or how you hope to function in a family unit. Challenging questions may come up, such as how your dating partner will feel about the pornography addiction you've struggled against and repented of, or how they will feel about your having a job that requires frequent travel. Those types of conversations will come if the relationship progresses, but in this step, focus primarily on the basics of the relationship. Don't ask too much of a relationship before giving it time to grow strong enough to support the weight of your request.

When you really like someone, it can be tempting to spill everything out of your heart at once. If you've waited a long time to date someone, you may need to remind yourself to take it slow. Oversharing, especially early on, can be too much too soon. Proverbs 14:10 states, "The heart knows its own bitterness, and no stranger shares its joy." Give the relationship time before opening up to this person about the deep parts of your heart.

Steps 3 to 6 overlap quite a bit, especially during seasons when you are transitioning from one phase to another. None of these steps should be seen as rigid categories that are totally separate and different.

Overall, it's helpful to remember that your main goal is not to marry this person but rather to find out if God wants you to marry them. If you discover at any point during these dating steps that God wants you to break up and not marry this person, that is a success, because you have gained clarity. If you go through all these dating steps and discover God wants you to proceed into marriage, that is a success too. The only true failure is to date someone you know God does not want you to date or to keep dating someone you know God is telling you to marry. You can review chapter 9 for more on this.

You need at least six months at step 3 to have time to enjoy the relationship and lay a good foundation. Step 4 may involve going through some hard things together, so you want to have a season of connecting first to build up the necessary emotional equity for what is to come.

Step 4. Moderately Serious Dating

Purpose: The goal of the moderately serious dating step is to address any potential relationship deal breakers before things get too serious. You don't need to know yet if God wants the two of you to marry, but it's time to actively investigate any potential barriers that may not have been obvious earlier.

Length: Of the total six-month to two-year guideline, this step usually lasts somewhere between one week and six months.

Commitment: On a scale of 1 to 10, this is a 4 or 5.

Additional Comments: With this season, the "honeymoon" phase of the dating relationship comes to an end. Ideally, the early stages of your relationship were great. You went on lots of dates, met each other's friends and family in casual settings, and saw clear evidence that you both like each other and fit well together. By this time, obvious theological differences, big life-pattern differences, and major personality differences should have already surfaced.

Now it's time to thoroughly assess each other and the realistic possibility of getting married. You don't need to be certain you want to marry each other yet, but you do want to start picking and prodding to make sure no deal breakers have gone unnoticed.

This is also the time to have any hard conversations you were keeping until the relationship was stronger. If there is anything in your past that someone would want to know before marrying you, now is the time to mention it.

It's best to wait until this phase to have these conversations, because you usually don't want to share deeply personal things with someone you don't know well. If you share sensitive information about yourself early on, and the two of you never make it out of the early dating phase for other reasons, you may come to regret revealing more of yourself than necessary.

However, you don't want to wait too long to drop a potential relationship bombshell. This can make the other person feel deceived, as if you let them get attached to you while withholding a key bit of information about what they were signing up for. Diving into these types of concerns during this step is usually the right timing because the two of you have built enough trust to be in a more serious relationship, and that's a sign you can probably trust the other person with more sensitive information about you.

Examples of things that might be relevant to reveal about yourself at this point include: poor financial decisions you've made in the past, carrying a significant amount of debt, having a medical condition that prevents you from having children, a former addiction to drugs or pornography, or a previous criminal record. There are countless examples of things that people don't need to know about you early on in a relationship but they do need to consider before choosing to marry you.

One of the reasons I put the length of this season as somewhere between a week and six months is because the variables that need to be considered can vary widely from couple to couple. A young couple may have little baggage to reveal to each other. Such a couple should still have at least one conversation during this phase to make sure they see themselves headed in the same general direction in life.

Another couple may be previously divorced and looking at blending two families, or any number of other variables. They will need more time to get on the same page, understand what they believe the Bible teaches about divorce and remarriage, and make sure they are both healed enough from the past to start something new. If they can't come to terms within about six months, however, this ongoing question mark may be a sign they should move on from each other. If more than six months are needed to determine if something is a deal breaker, it's probably best to assume it is, rather than continuing to wish things were different.

All that to say, somewhere between the relationship phases of "not too serious" and "very serious" is when you should have these types of hard conversations with your boyfriend or girlfriend.

Step 5. Serious Dating

Purpose: The goal of the serious dating step is to begin to depend on this person in deeper ways to really test whether you can faithfully love each other in marriage. Whether through moving closer to engagement or breaking up, your goal is to bring this relationship to a point of decision.

Length: Around three to six months.

Commitment: On a scale of 1 to 10, you are around a 6 or 7.

Additional Comments: So far in this hypothetical dating relationship, we've focused mostly on connecting and assessing. At this point, we add *depending* to the equation. Talk of dependence can evoke a wide array of emotions. Some people say, "Of course you should depend on your boyfriend or girlfriend! What's the point of being together if you can't depend on each other!" Other people might say, "No, depend on Christ alone. No human can fill your heart. Only Jesus has what you need!"

Both arguments, even stated in the extreme, have valid points. But the confusion comes from not realizing we're talking about two different things. In one sense, you can and should only depend on Jesus. Even in marriage, your spouse can't meet your heart's deepest needs. Only God's perfect love can satisfy your need for perfect love.

But if you never allow yourself to depend on your dating partner, you wall your heart off from them. No, we shouldn't depend on any human in the ultimate sense. Only God can be depended on like that. But when it comes to relationships, depending on each other is essential for true love (Gal. 6:1–5).

Dating makes this question about dependence especially complicated, because if you start depending on someone too much too soon, you will put more weight on the commitment than it can handle. If you make your new boyfriend or girlfriend feel like their future is already planned out, you may freak them out, because you seem more committed than they are. They may even back away in fear of leading you on. But if you never depend on your boyfriend or girlfriend, you will never know if you can thrive together in marriage. And who wants to marry someone you can't depend on?

So, after dealing with any hard conversations in step 4 and acknowledging things are getting pretty serious, it's time to start putting weight on the relationship to see if it can handle the stress. If your partner cannot reciprocate the love and openness you show them, it's best to learn this before marrying them.

This needs to be done carefully, because when you start depending on someone and opening your heart to them, your emotions and sexual desire for them are likely to increase as well. This is natural and why I believe in keeping this season pretty short. After three to six months of being in a serious dating relationship, things are going to get too deep for dating.

If the relationship continues to thrive at this point in your dating journey, it's time to move toward engagement.

Step 6. Pre-Engagement

Purpose: The goal of the pre-engagement step is to get God's final word about the relationship. You need to feel confident about God's plan for you and this person, because it's decision time—get engaged or accept it isn't meant to be and break up.

Length: One week to two months.

Commitment: On a scale of 1 to 10, you are around an 8.

Additional Comments: It would be easy to lump this into step 5, but at the climax of a serious dating relationship, I believe it is important to take one last step back and fully decide what God is saying to you before actually getting engaged.

I'm not saying you should emotionally back away from your boyfriend or girlfriend or that you should take a break from each other or anything like that. I'm just advocating that you take some time to clear your mind and heart, quiet yourself before the Lord, and hear what he is saying to you about your future with this person. Perhaps you should set aside extra prayer time, fast, go on a short spiritual retreat, or ask others to pray with you so you can get an abundance of confirmation about what God is leading you to do.

At this point in your dating journey, engagement is right around the corner. Some of you may wonder why this wasn't done a long time ago. Why not ask God for absolute clarity earlier in your journey? Shoot, why not ask him as soon as you meet someone for the first time, "Lord, is this person the one?"

The reason I encourage you to seek God's clear word at this point in your relationship is because you now have the necessary history and evidence for God to answer this question for you. By now, if you have followed the first five steps, you have seen everything you need to see in real life to confirm what you sense God saying to you in your heart. If you ask God if this person is the one before you have had time to gather tangible evidence through which God can answer this question for you, there is a strong probability you could mishear God in your prayer time, allowing yourself to hear what you want rather than the truth.

It's true you should always be praying for clarity as you date this person. But before you decide to ask a woman to marry you or accept a man's engagement request, you should make sure you feel confident that you are hearing God's clear answer to you.

Besides the obvious reason of wanting to do this so you can properly follow God and not marry someone he is warning you not to marry, this step also gives you peace. If God is telling you to marry this person but you never slow down enough to really feel it in your heart, you will lack the peace God desires for you. Even if God is saying yes, you won't feel at ease until you know you are hearing God say yes to you.

You can date someone without being sure God wants you to marry them, but never get engaged without being confident you are hearing God accurately. If you aren't sure yet, you may need some more time to date. If you are getting close to three or four years in your dating relationship, and you still are unclear if you should marry this person, it's worth considering that God's answer might be not to marry this person. God may be telling you no, and you have been unwilling to hear it. Dating endlessly is unwise and almost always leads to sin. God never wants you to do anything that would hurt your walk with him.

In short, eventually a serious dating relationship needs to end. Either break up or get engaged.

Step 7. Engagement

Purpose: Your goal in the engagement step is to make the necessary arrangements for you two to become husband and wife. Plan the wedding, figure out your living situation, and make it happen!

Length: One day to six months.

Commitment: On a scale of 1 to 10, you are at a 9.

Additional Comments: All your key questions about this person should now be answered. You will still learn new things about your partner as you grow as a couple. There are still unknowns. But the questions you needed to have answered before stepping into the unknown future with this person as a married couple have been answered.

Your goal is no longer to find clarity. You've found it. Your goal now is to get married. Americans, in most cases, get this season way wrong. It's not uncommon to hear about people being engaged for years. This is a big mistake biblically, because engagement is still not marriage in God's eyes. Planning the perfect wedding isn't worth falling into sin. Don't let the idolatry of one day spoil the true significance of getting married for the glory of God.

As I've said, anywhere from six months to two years is plenty of time to reach engagement. Once you're engaged, tack on no more than an additional six months. The sooner you can get married at this point, the better! In most cases, a prolonged engagement makes little sense. It can easily lead to sexual sin, since you will feel practically married even though you are not. If you have things to work through before you can get married, or you aren't sure if you really want to get married, don't get engaged. Once you get engaged, you should move quickly to marriage.

It is far better to rush through engagement than to prolong it. Never rush *getting* engaged. Don't say yes to someone if you have unanswered questions. Keep dating until you find the answers or realize you will never find the answers and thus you need to break up. But once you have decided to marry this person and you have done your due diligence to get God's confirmation about your future marriage, eloping is healthier than staying engaged for years.

I'm not encouraging you to elope. I'm just saying it's less damaging to rush getting married at this point than delaying getting married. You should involve your local church in your wedding ceremony, and your friends and family deserve to be blessed by witnessing what God is doing in your relationship for his glory. But don't play with fire. Your passion for each other at this point should be almost uncontrollable, if you are properly resisting each other like the Bible instructs.

But you are not married yet. So if God reveals something to you during this time or you realize you've made a mistake by saying you would marry this person, it's not too late to back out. It may be embarrassing and hurtful to your fiancé, but in some situations, it is the right thing to do.

In summary, if you know this is your future spouse, why wait? Get it done and enjoy your marriage together!

Step 8. Wedding Vows

Purpose: The goal of the wedding vows step is to officially become a husband and wife through making the ultimate commitment to each other. You are committing before God and a watching world that you intend to glorify God through loving each other in marriage.

Length: 1 to 10 minutes.

Commitment: On a scale of 1 to 10, you are at a 10.

Additional Comments: A wedding ceremony is saturated with culture. The clothes, the music, and many of the actions performed are completely personal choices. You do you! But when it comes to the vows, may I offer you my opinion?

Keep them simple.

You may want to make endless promises to this special person on this special day. And behind those promises you will have nothing but pure intentions. But just know, you will fail so often as a married couple. Nothing has humbled me more than my own inability to love Bethany perfectly like I want to. No one ever lives up to the ideal we all hope to attain when we dream about marriage. Therefore, it's unwise and dangerous to make lavish vows.

Further, vows should not be taken lightly: "Make your vows to the LORD your God and perform them" (Ps. 76:11). It diminishes the marriage vows when we promise unattainable things. However, it is possible to make vows on your wedding day that you can deliver on.

You can't promise to never say anything mean, to never take this person for granted, and to always give them everything they want in life. But you can promise to be faithful no matter what you two go through. You can promise to honor your commitment to this person to always be their husband or to always be their wife. It's trendy to write your own vows. It's certainly not a sin to do so. But I'm personally a big fan of traditional marriage vows, because they capture the essence of what you can truly vow to do.

Jesus is our Savior. You can't be your future spouse's savior, nor can they be yours. But the two of you can be faithful till death do you part as you seek to bear the image of God's faithfulness for this glory. As Hebrews 13:4–5 says:

> Let marriage be held in honor among all, and let the marriage bed be undefiled, for God will judge the sexually immoral and adulterous. Keep your life free from love of money, and be content with what you have, for he has said, "I will never leave you nor forsake you."

12

CHRIST OVER COMPATIBILITY

A huge part of me wants to leave you on a high note and tell you that Bethany and I lived happily ever after. In most ways, this is true. We have been very happy together. But I am a work in progress, as is Bethany. Our relationship will always be a work in progress.

We have had highlights and continue to experience amazing times together. I could easily fill these closing pages with romantic stories from our marriage—our honeymoon in Glacier National Park; how we found our first dog, a beautiful red golden retriever named Lois Lane; how Bethany let me know she was pregnant with our children, Logan and Noel; fruitful ministry; adventurous vacations; laughter with our children; growing in a healthy Christian community with others; new houses; career advancements; and so much more. I can say with a clean conscience that we have a very good marriage that is deepening every year by the grace of God.

But our sin is also real. We've hurt each other deeply. I know these are vague statements, so please understand, we haven't murdered anyone, committed adultery, or done anything that would biblically justify divorce. Every couple struggles with unique temptations. Bethany and I don't struggle in areas where some other couples do—and we do struggle in ways some other couples don't.

To keep it authentic but also general, I'll put it like this: Bethany and I have really struggled with managing our anger and using our words wisely during seasons of stress. Day to day, we are very respectful toward each other. But over the years, we've had seasons of trials that strained our marriage in extreme ways.

When we had our second child, Noel, Logan was two years old. Some parents transition easily from one child to two. Not us. It took some time for us to adapt to having even less sleep. Just when we thought we had things figured out, the kids' needs would change. Then when Noel was one and Logan was three, I had a major career change, and we were forced to rebuild financially. During this season, as soon as we felt like we could come up for air, another wave would crash over us. Our love never wavered, but we were running on empty, and it showed in how we communicated during disagreements.

You can't retrieve words you've spoken. You can say you didn't mean them and receive forgiveness, but you can't unsay them. In seconds, words can rip through a relationship, causing damage that takes months to repair. I hate to admit it, but we've yelled at each other. We've been unjustly angry for stupid reasons. We've acted selfishly because we didn't take time to listen. We got to a point one time where we couldn't see clearly, and so we worked with a marriage counselor to get out of the fog we were in. By God's grace, we've forgiven each other every time. We've grown a lot as individuals and as a couple. We continue to find things to work on.

The key to experiencing the true beauty of marriage is commitment in the midst of trials. We can still love each other, even after seeing both of us at our worst, because God has provided us with deep grace for each other through the deep commitment he has given us. Without the commitment of marriage, we would not have experienced the grace we have in our relationship. Even when sin occurs, God has helped us see each other for who we are in Christ. Bethany knows my sin nature better than anyone, but she also knows my new nature in Christ better than anyone. I can say the same for her.

The pain of marriage, if you make it through together, allows you to experience deeper love than you ever thought possible. The reason for its depth, though, is because you went through darker days than you ever thought possible. Love deepens because of hardships, not in spite of them.

Again, the sunny days are amazing too! We've had many seasons in our marriage where things felt perfect. But it's because of hard times that we can experience more good times together. As it says in James 1:2–4, "Count it all joy, my brothers, when you meet trials of various kinds, for you know that the testing of your faith produces steadfastness. And let steadfastness have its full effect, that you may be perfect and complete, lacking in nothing."

Every couple goes through different trials. Deep love and affection grow when you fight through the hard times together without quitting. The easy times can't fuel the commitment. Your commitment to God and each other allows you to endure the storms and stand together when the sun begins to shine on your faces once more (Ps. 37:5–6).

Bethany is downstairs right now with a close friend who is in town visiting family. She and her husband have three children, between the ages of eight and sixteen. Recently, she called Bethany, joyfully, to tell her she was pregnant again. We were all so excited for her and her family. Sadly, a few days ago, she called Bethany again, sorrowfully, to say she'd had a miscarriage. Their family is heartbroken and grieving their loss.

Yesterday, after church, we went to lunch with an older couple we've known for years, whose children are grown. We love spending time with them, since they've been through all the seasons we are in right now. They are two of the most mature Christians I know. A few years ago, their oldest son was diagnosed with cancer. Last year, he passed away at the age of twenty.

What will you do in moments like these? Will tragedy tear you apart, or will it bring you even closer? How will you respond when things happen in your marriage that you wish didn't happen? How will you choose to keep loving your spouse when you see their sin nature in clearer ways than you ever thought possible? How will you stay present and not run away when they see your sin? How will you deal with the stress parenthood will put on your marriage? How will you react if your child gets cancer? How will you face your fears that no one else understands?

Love deepens because of hardships, not in spite of them.

These are not the dreams Christian singles have for marriage. Yes, most of us know intellectually ahead of time that marriage is hard. I knew this too, because I had heard enough couples say it. But I didn't *feel* this truth until I experienced it for myself. Knowing something and experiencing it are very different.

Marriage is way more brutal than we imagine, because when you have another person around all the time, it is impossible to hide. I can hide things from you, because I edit my videos and only share what I want to share in my writing. I can hide things from friends, because after we hang out, we all go home. But I can't hide my flaws from Bethany. I may have been successful for a short period of time, but if you live with someone long enough, the sin nature always makes an appearance.

Not that marriage is all doom and gloom. But we don't really need any help getting through the easy parts. Just enjoy them—don't idolize them—and praise God for them! What we need help with are the hard days. Hopefully they are much fewer than the good days, but no matter who you are, the storms always come eventually. And if you are not prepared, they can destroy everything you cherish (Matt. 7:24–27).

Storms are temporary, but if your home isn't weatherproof, they can be devastating. This is true in marriage too. Hard times won't last forever, but if you aren't prepared for them, they can ruin the relationship for good. So it is crucial that Christian singles know that, yes, sunny days will be there, but storms will come too. How you deal with storms will determine whether your marriage survives long term.

Years ago, Bethany and I were out to dinner with a couple we were just getting to know. He was a paramedic on the east side of

Cleveland, a very rough part of town. At one point, trying to make conversation, I asked playfully, "What's the craziest thing you've seen as a paramedic?" The man paused, as though a dark memory was emerging, and then said something so graphic and dark that I won't repeat it here. I immediately knew I had a naive view of the trauma a paramedic sees while working in one of the most violent cities in America. In this case, being naive had little impact on me, but when Christian singles are naive about the hard times in marriage, it can cause them to be dangerously unprepared for the trials ahead.

As I said, I'd prefer not to share the hard times with you. I'd rather focus on all the wins. But my conscience won't allow that, because that's probably not what serves you best. It would be irresponsible of me to spray you with glitter and confetti as we part ways, rather than speak the truth. Selfishly, I might have chosen to talk about the romantic things I've planned over the years, the amazing gifts Bethany has given me, and the increasing health our marriage has experienced as we've worked hard on it together. My ego would love it if you saw Bethany and me as your "relationship goal." But honestly, that wouldn't help you at all. You probably have enough mental images about the coming joys of marriage. I don't want to expand the gap that may already exist between your expectations and the realities of marriage.

You and your future spouse may not struggle with anger and saying hurtful words, like Bethany and I have at times, but you will encounter struggles that you don't expect. So rather than talk about the joys of marriage, which you *will* undoubtedly experience if you get married, I want to talk more about the need for Christ in your future marriage.

Christ is the answer in both the good times and the bad.

Personal Compatibility for Christ's Sake

Remember, this isn't a book about marriage. It's about *glorifying God* through pursuing marriage. With that in mind, let's talk about how you should prepare in singleness, as you seek to meet, date, and marry the person God has for you.

On the topic of compatibility, there are two extreme views among Christians. One view says compatibility doesn't matter because a godly marriage is all about commitment. The other view emphasizes compatibility and equates minor differences with being unequally yoked. I advocate for reasonable compatibility with unreasonable commitment. With these two goals, we can accomplish the desires Christ has for us in marriage. He wants marriage to be enjoyable, so we can show the world how he enjoys his church, and he wants it to be a witness to the world of his commitment to his church.

Unreasonable Commitment

Let's start with *unreasonable commitment*, since that is probably the least-understood phrase. Most of us have been taught from our youth to treat everyone fairly. If you bring snacks for some classmates, you have to bring enough for the whole class. In job interviews, the law requires that no one be treated unfairly because of race or religious beliefs. At the voting booth, all votes are weighted equally, regardless of economic and social standing. If we break the law, justice is supposed to be blind, and we are to be punished fairly, not too much, nor too little for the crime. A just society, at its best, is fair.

God, however, does not treat us fairly. If God treated us fairly, we would all be in hell right now, because that's what our sins deserve (Rom. 6:23). God treats us better than fair: "He does not deal with us according to our sins, nor repay us according to our iniquities" (Ps. 103:10). When David finally repented of his sins with Bathsheba, he pleaded with God to treat him according to God's character, not David's own character: "Have mercy on me, O God, according to your steadfast love; according to your abundant mercy blot out my transgressions" (Ps. 51:1).

The gospel is not reasonable. It is very unreasonable. Jesus treats his church so unfairly. He loves us so much more than we deserve. If we could lose God's love and faithfulness, we would have lost it already. Thankfully, God's love and commitment are not rooted in our deservedness but in his nature. God loves unconditionally because "God is love" (1 John 4:16). He remains faithful and committed to his church because he is faithful and committed in his nature: "If we are faithless, he remains faithful—for he cannot deny himself" (2 Tim. 2:13).

If your goal is to glorify God in marriage by reflecting God's image in marriage, you must prepare in singleness to have an unfair, unreasonable commitment to your future spouse.

Reasonable Compatibility

But your marriage, if you marry, will be based in part on *reasonable compatibility.* Since marriage is a biblical option, not a biblical command, it's unbiblical to think that God will command you to marry someone you don't enjoy. Compatibility is an important factor in enjoyment. Not that you will enjoy your future spouse every moment of the day. But God does not expect you to marry someone you don't want to marry.

We should learn to love and embrace all people. When we go to church, the pews should be full of all types of people. We'll more naturally get along better with some than others. Still, we should learn to love and be there for one another as we seek to reflect the unity God wants his church to have (Phil. 2:1–11). You won't want to live with everyone you meet at church. You won't be best friends with all the members in your congregation. But you can all still choose to be one in Christ by glorifying him together.

The gospel is not reasonable. It is very unreasonable. Jesus treats his church so unfairly. He loves us so much more than we deserve.

Marriage is different, however. You should want to live with your future spouse and enjoy being around them. You should only choose to marry someone you really want to marry. Therefore, you should expect to have common interests so you can easily enjoy parts of your life together. If you are extremely introverted, and someone you initially liked is so extroverted you need a break after ten minutes with them, you should not feel compelled to overlook this glaring compatibility issue. Compatibility is good.

The problem occurs when we have unreasonable compatibility demands. We all have different personality temperaments. If you are high in agreeableness, you can more easily enjoy someone who is very different from you. If you are low in agreeableness, you may struggle with enjoying those who are different from you and find greater enjoyment with people who are similar to you in personal interests and tastes. Being low or high in agreeableness is not better or worse. It's just how God made us. We need to be respectful and loving to everyone, but each of us has different tolerance levels for being with people with varying views and interests.

I won't give you a concrete rule about the ideal degree of compatibility for a healthy relationship. I will simply encourage you to be reasonable. If you are a man who loves basketball, maybe don't put "Must love basketball" at the top of your wish list. If you are a woman who loves music, it's okay if your future husband isn't a musician like you. Why? Because things like basketball and music are not essential for a glorifying, enjoyable marriage. It's great if you do find someone who checks every box on your list, but don't expect this. Rather, focus on the bigger question, *Do I enjoy this person?*

In addition to personal enjoyment, look for compatibility in general life direction. For example, if God is calling you to be a missionary, you will want to look for someone who is at least open to such a calling. While this isn't a biblical issue, since you can glorify God wherever you live, it does impact your compatibility if you marry someone who wants a different lifestyle than you.

Perhaps you want to have a lot of children, both biological and adopted. This is good. But not everyone will feel the same way. Some people may want only one or two children and prefer not to adopt. If God has called you to have a big family, but you are dating someone who is strongly opposed to this, neither of you are biblically wrong, because the Bible doesn't give us an exact number of children we must produce through marriage. But this is a practical issue that indicates you may not be compatible enough for marriage.

When it comes to personal compatibility, you're looking for two things. First, you need to enjoy being with this person. Second, you need to be willing to go in the same basic direction in life. At times, you will get annoyed with each other. You will sometimes have different desires and need to compromise. No two people are 100 percent compatible. But *generally*, you should enjoy each other and be on the same page about the direction of your lives.

If you find someone you enjoy and can travel through life with, that's all the personal compatibility you need.

Theological Compatibility for Christ's Sake

As you may have noticed, I've been focusing on *personal* compatibility. This is different from *theological* compatibility. With regard to theological compatibility, we should be more rigid than we are with personal compatibility.

It can be difficult to know what theological differences are deal breakers for a relationship. In determining theological compatibility, I've found it helpful to categorize your differences into three main tiers.

Tier One: Salvation Issues

Tier one topics are a matter of salvation. Any theological doctrine that separates Christians from non-Christians is in this tier. Examples of tier one issues include topics like the Trinity, salvation by grace alone through faith alone, the historical reality of Jesus, the divinity of Jesus, and the fact that there is one true gospel.

Because the Bible requires Christians to only marry other Christians (1 Cor. 7:39; 2 Cor. 6:14), and because tier one topics are salvation issues, I believe the Bible requires Christians to only marry people who are compatible in these areas. If you are not theologically compatible here, you are not one in Christ, which is what a husband and wife are called to be.

So if you are a Christian and therefore believe in the Trinity, and the person you are dating believes Jesus is the son of God but not divine, thus denying the Trinity, you should not marry this person, because you are not theologically compatible. Or if someone said they believe the Bible is just a moral book that explains one possible way to salvation, but you believe the Bible is perfect in every way and proclaims the truth that Jesus is the one way to be saved, this would be a tier one difference, and you should not marry this person.

Tier Two: Important Theological Subjects

Tier two topics are important theological subjects, but people can have different opinions on them and still be considered Christians. Topics in this category affect the way we live and the church we attend. While these issues are important, Christians who disagree are usually still willing to consider one another brothers and sisters in Christ. Examples of topics that fall into this category are beliefs about baptism and communion, divorce and remarriage, female or male-only pastors, and church governance.

I recommend finding someone you are theologically compatible with on tier two beliefs. It will be difficult to enjoy each other and head in the same general life direction—especially when raising children together—if you disagree on these types of topics. While I think it's usually unwise to marry someone with tier two theological differences, I don't consider it sinful or unbiblical to marry such a person. I believe interfaith marriages are sinful for Christians. I believe interdenominational marriages for Christians are usually unwise, but not sinful.

It's clear the Bible requires Christians to only marry other Christians. It's unclear how theologically compatible we need to be. I think you can be equally yoked if you disagree with someone about an important theological topic as long as you both agree on the gospel (Gal. 1:8–9). However, a difference in beliefs about a tier two issue can easily lead to significant conflicts in marriage and greatly diminish your enjoyment of marriage. Beliefs dictate actions. If your beliefs are very different, you will constantly be pulling in two different ways.

Tier Three: Debatable but Not Divisive Issues

Tier three topics are issues that people may enjoy discussing and debating but do not significantly impact their ability to get along with one another. Topics addressed in the Bible that don't fall into tier one or two are tier three topics. These are important topics that people in the same church or denomination may disagree on, but they still choose to work together.

A common example of a tier three issue is your preference of Bible translation. I really like the ESV. You may really like the NIV. Others may read the NLT. While these versions contain significant differences that are important to know about, we can all attend the same church and not get hung up arguing over which translation is better.

A good rule of thumb is, if you both could be members at the same church, you are probably theologically compatible enough for marriage. If you are having a theological difference with someone but the issue in question doesn't really affect the way you live your life or the church you attend, you can still marry this person and be very theologically compatible.

There are a lot of tier three issues in life. When you are considering marrying someone, don't expect them to see every biblical issue exactly as you do. Don't let these smaller differences stop you from uniting with another true believer in marriage as a witness to the world of God's glory (John 17:22–23).

If you want to glorify God through marriage, you must prepare to love like Christ loves. He is not faithful because we deserve it. His fullness fuels his faithfulness for us. He doesn't love in response to our love for him. He's not responding in a reactionary way like we do in our human interactions. His actions flow out of his heart and being.

Likewise, our love and commitment in marriage must flow out of our fullness in God, not out of perfect compatibility with our spouse. As Christ loves his church out of his fullness rather than need, so too must we drink deeply of God's love so we can pour much love into our spouse. If a husband and wife are drawing from each other, both will go empty. God is the endless well of love, thus we must draw our love from him.

Christ will empower us to reveal God's character through giving radical love, not through finding someone just like us.

Every "How" Will Be Accomplished through the Ultimate "Why"

Our goal for this study was to answer the question "How can you glorify God through your pursuit of marriage?"

We started by defining what it means to glorify God. Through studying "the glory of God" in the context of Scripture, we learned that to glorify him we must reveal his image accurately. Because Jesus makes the invisible God visible (John 1:14; Col. 1:15; Heb. 1:3), the best way to glorify God is to proclaim the gospel truth about Jesus Christ through our words and deeds (2 Cor. 4:4–6).

We then applied this knowledge about glorifying God to the specific topic of glorifying him through pursuing marriage. If we want to make the character of God known through proclaiming Jesus Christ accurately in our dating efforts, we must date in a way that resembles the character of Christ. Thus, this book is called *Christ-Centered Dating: Pursuing a Relationship That Glorifies God.* Or to say it slightly differently, the way you glorify God through your pursuit of marriage is to date in a Christ-centered way.

Next, we talked about practical ways to do this. In Ephesians 5:21–33, we are taught that a husband and wife are called to reflect Christ and the church in the relationship. Applying marriage principles to dating, we concluded it was best for a man to pursue the woman, as Christ pursues the church; it's best for the woman to invite and respond to the man's pursuit as the church invites and responds to Jesus' pursuit.

We also discussed some specific methods a man and woman can use to connect with and assess each other to guard their hearts throughout the dating phases. Whether it be through dating, courting, or my hybrid approach, the goal of your dating journey should not be to marry this person at any cost, but rather to learn what God's will is for you both. Clarity, not marriage, must be your main goal for dating.

If you find someone you enjoy and can travel through life with, that's all the personal compatibility you need.

Finally, in this chapter, I've done my best to prepare you for the future marriage God might have for you by showing you the importance of valuing oneness in Christ over surface-level compatibility. The radical commitment you need to thrive in marriage is unreasonable from a worldly standpoint. However, to glorify God in marriage, your faithfulness will need to far exceed what is reasonable in the world's eyes. It must be radical, not rational; for God's love for us is not rational. It is radical and never-ending.

In these final pages, I want to close where we began this study, remembering the centrality of God's glory. No matter what happens once you close this book, remember this: God's glorification must always be your goal.

Not only does God deserve to be glorified, but glorifying him is what is best for us. God made us for the purpose of glorifying him. When we misplace our purpose, when the meaning of our lives becomes a mystery, our lack of clarity affects the way we live. This is true when it comes to relationships as well. As we talked about in chapter 2, why you want to get married will guide how you pursue marriage.

In other words, when you have the right *why*, you can accomplish any *how*. How will you overcome your desire to project past wounds onto future relationships? How will you deal with loving someone who isn't like the person you imagined in your head when you dreamed about "the one"? How will you reject the pressure from your friends and family to date in a worldly way? And how will you find solutions to all the questions you still have that I did not address in this book?

This is when you must remember your why. Instead of starting with how, start by asking why. Why should you overcome your desire to project past wounds onto future relationships? Why should you deal with the confusion caused by loving someone who isn't like the person you imagined in your head when you dreamed about "the one"? Why should you reject the pressure from your friends and family to date in a worldly way? And why should you even try to find solutions to all the questions you still have that I did not address in this book?

The answer must be—for God's glory.

Christ will empower us to reveal God's character through giving radical love, not through finding someone just like us.

There are a million little tricks and tips about relationships that can help along the way. There are countless other biblical principles we could discuss. But if you have the correct why, you have the solution to any how that might come your way.

I can't predict what your dating journey will look like. I don't know what your future marriage will entail, what hardships await, or what happiness is in store for you. Each of our stories will be different. And yet, if you take hold of the ultimate why, God will give you the grace to figure out whatever how comes your way.

Therefore, the path forward for all of us, no matter what happens, is to glorify God.